Modern Custom Knives

The Great Collections

Modern Custom Knives

The Great Collections

Dr. David Darom

Series producer
Paolo Saviolo

Photography
**Eric Eggly, PointSeven Studios, Inc.
Francesco Pachì**

CHARTWELL
BOOKS, INC.

All texts were written by the artists and edited by Dr. David Darom

Photography:
The photographers whose work is depicted throughout this book hold the copyrights to the images they created. They authorized the author to digitally manipulate the original backgrounds, creating new ones for the book.

Digital image processing: Dr. David Darom and Nir Darom

Book Design: Nomi Morag, Jerusalem, Israel
Copyeditor: Evelyn Katrak, Jerusalem, Israel
Color conversions: Ya'acov Laloum, Jerusalem, Israel
Indigo proofs: Panorama Ltd., Jerusalem, Israel. info@panorama.co.il

© 2007 White Star S.p.A.
Via Candido Sassone, 22/24
13100 Vercelli, Italy
www.whitestar.it

This edition published in 2008 by
CHARTWELL BOOKS, INC.
A division of BOOK SALES, INC.
114 Northfield Avenue
Edison, New Jersey 08837
USA

ISBN 13: 978-0-7858-2360-5
ISBN 10: 0-7858-2360-3

REPRINTS:
1 2 3 4 5 6   12 11 10 09 08
Printed in China

Front cover from the left:
Kenneth King, USA, "Eye of God", 2006, From the collection of Jeff Gale, USA. see page 64
Van Barnett and Dellana, USA, "Golden Heart", 2007, From the collection of Gerald Hopkin, Barbados, see page 122

Back cover from the left:
Steve R. Johnson, USA, 4 one-of-a-kind knives with 4 different logos.
"Milano Knife", 2000, Made to celebrate SRJ's first time participation in the Milan Knife Show. Special logo with the map of Italy. Ten gold tubes in the polished stag handle. Overall length 9 7/8" (251 mm).
"01-01-01 Dirk", 2001, Steve's first knife for 2001. Mother-of-Pearl handle and the date "01-01-01" in the logo. Overall length 9 7/16" (240 mm).
"Vertical Logo Knife", 2001, The only knife made by SRJ with a vertical logo. Pre-ban elephant ivory handle. Overall length 9 3/8" (238 mm).
"Calendar Knife", 1991, Mammoth ivory handle. Overall length 8 1/2" (215 mm).
All knives from the collection of Dr. Pierluigi Peroni, Italy.

Title page, from the left:
Reinhard Tschager, Italy, Three fixed-blade pocket "Jewel Knives", especially made for the collector with his "PLP" monogram. All three knives engraved by Valerio Peli (Italy).
"Symmetrical Dagger", 2004, Integral guard with gold inlays, engraved blade and Black-lip pearl inlays in the handle. Overall length 4 15/16" (125 mm).
"Semi-Integral Drop", 2003, Engraved guard and ancient tortoise shell handle. Overall length 4 3/4" (121 mm).
"Mini Integral", 2001, Very first "Jewel knife" made by Tschager. Engraved gold insert in the premium Mother-of-Pearl handle. Overall length 4 3/8" (106 mm).
All knives from the collection of Dr. Pierluigi Peroni, Italy.

First published in a limited edition of 1250 copies, June 2007

Table of Contents

Preface

Opposite page, from the top:
Dr. Fred Carter, USA
"Four Knife Set", 2006
Four elephant ivory handled knives
tied together as a set with matching
engraving. This commissioned set
consists of two large hunting knives
and two smaller skinning knives. The
topmost knife was fashioned from
AHT-24, a Japanese steel given to
Dr. Carter by Mr. Akihisa Kawasaki
(1926-2005). This steel was a special
melt steel that was used by Kawasaki
in his very original line of handmade
knives. It is especially tough even in the
annealed state and as such is difficult
to work with and even more difficult
to engrave. The blade was ground and
hand finished, relief engraved and
then heat treated. The bolsters and
ivory handles were then attached,
shaped and polished, followed by the
relief engraving of the bolsters. *"When
drawing this knife I tried to keep in
mind the memory of my old friend, Mr.
Kawasaki and his wonderfully designed
knives - more than once he said to me,
'design is everything'".*
Overall length 8" (203 mm).
The second knife was fashioned from
ATS-34 stainless steel. The blade was
hand finished and handled with ivory.
This particular knife is a design that
appeared in Dr. Carter's original 1976
catalog of knives, which was used in his
application to the Knifemakers Guild that
same year. Overall length 8" (203 mm).
The third and fourth knives are smaller
skinning knives both with ivory and
ATS-34 steel. Overall lengths 7 1/8" (181
mm) and 6 3/4" (171 mm).

The world of custom knives will never be the same for me after
exploring it in depth over the past five years and ending up with
4 magnificent books standing on my bookshelf. Gazing at these
four volumes, there are moments when I catch myself daydreaming
and wondering how on earth I took upon myself to even consider
dealing with such a major undertaking. A five-year intensively
time-consuming process that was created on my Macintosh, at
home, ended way beyond the simple "dream come true" stage as
it turned into a 1072 page, four volume art-book series dedicated
to modern custom knives. Then come those moments when I feel
deeply thankful to have somehow found the strength to pull it
all off and see my original concept become a reality. Strength
constantly bestowed onto me, by many friends from around the
world as well as family close by.

The time that I actually invested in producing these four
art books - about 7000 hours of "production" work plus 16 trips
to knife shows in far away lands - does not truly indicate the
stressful events involved in desperately clinging to deadlines or the
hundreds of sleepless nights that go with this. Nor does it give any
idea about the tremendous pressure that develops while working
with more than 200 knifemakers, photographers, collectors, knife
dealers, designers and printers during an almost non-stop period
of five years. And it was not just working with so many from all
around the globe, it was, in many cases, getting involved with
some of their personal problems too. Advising and suggesting as
well as coaching them, nagging, pushing and working with them
on-line, sometimes for hours at a time. Another one of the daring
aspects, maybe the most amazing aspect of this adventure, was that
in many cases I had not even met the people represented in my
books! At first I only got to know them by means of Internet and
long phone conversations, meeting most of them eventually for
the first time, only after the books were published and introduced
to the public... I think it is quite in place to repeat here part of
what I said in 2002, for the epilogue of my first book "Art and

Edmund Davidson, USA

"20th Anniversary Knife", 2006

This Full-Integral knife is #1 of
5 made to commemorate Edmund's
20 years of custom knifemaking. The
design for the 4" (102 mm) blade
was taken after the Bob Loveless
Nessmuck skinner pattern. The handle
is Edmund's *B. C. Skinner* design. Steel
is new CPM 154-CM and the handle
material is double-dyed (green and
black) and stabilized box elder wood.
Engraving is all hand cut by Jere
Davidson.
Overall length 8 7/8" (225 mm).

"David Darom's Subhilt", 2006

This recently created Full-Integral
Subhilt hunter model is named after
the author. Steel is 440-C and the
handle material is dyed and stabilized
box elder wood. Engraving is all hand
cut by Jere Davidson.
Overall length 10 3/16" (259 mm).

Edmund Davidson's art of making
Integral knives will be the subject
for the first book in a new series Dr.
David Darom is now creating. This
series, *"Great Custom
Knifemakers of the World"*, will
display the knifemaking processes
and many of the knives made by
the world-class custom knife artist
to whom each book is dedicated.
The plan is to produce 112-page
hard cover art books dedicated to
individual knifemakers, providing
an in depth study of their work for
generations to come.
The first volume will be:

*"Edmund Davidson -
The Art of the Integral Knife".*

The book will be introduced to the
public at the June 2008 Blade Show
held in Atlanta (USA).

Design in Modern Custom Folding Knives". It was so true then,
five years ago, and it says it all again, now, after finishing the
fourth volume...

*"Once there was a man who had a dream... Little did he
realize what was needed to get a selected group of artists from the
around the world to cooperate and work as a team. Little did he
imagine what it would take to get them doing 'extra-curricular'
work, sticking religiously to fixed timetables and deadlines. Little
could he visualize, although he himself gladly spent over 12
hours each day working on his dream, that these busy people
would also have other things on their minds. And, little did he
understand how nearly impossible it would be to follow this
vision through from over 10,000 miles away.... But, luckily for
us all, there was also much love and faith involved, and that is
what finally pulled it off".*

I cannot even begin to describe the great relationships
that developed over these years while working with so many
representatives of the art knife community. Friendships that were
created with knifemakers, custom knife related artists, collectors,
dealers and photographers from all around the world. These were
based on much more than the professional respect that occurs
while working together on a mutual project. It was more than just
sharing a passion for this beautiful art form. It was, in many cases,
a true friendship that flourished and linked our lives together.

There is no doubt about the fact that this fourth volume,
exhibiting highlights of some of the major western modern custom
knife collections, is first and foremost a tribute to the collectors
themselves. It is mainly because of their relentless promoting of
this art and the people that create it, that custom knifemaking has
reached the level where it is today.

Creating the last volume in this series in order to exhibit some
of the greatest treasures of contemporary custom knifemaking,
that are usually hidden away from any sort of public viewing,
was something for which I had to first build-up a good reputation.
Lucky for me I managed to do this using my first three books as
references, proving to everyone my dedication to the subject. My
first books on custom knives also helped me show my ability
to produce a series of art books of the highest standard in their
contents, visual presentation and finished product quality. I was
even more lucky when I got the full support of many makers,
collectors and art knife dealers who spoke highly about me and of
what I am doing for this art and its industry. Of these, the first and

foremost supporters were **Dave Nittinger** and **Phil Lobred**, without whose help I doubt that I could have been convincing enough to persuade the owners of the greatest custom knife collections to expose the contents of their safes to the public through me. When eventually this basic barrier was overcome, working on the book began with the recruited talents of two designated world-class photographers who used digital photography of the highest quality available. **Eric Eggly** of PointSeven Inc. was in charge of North America while **Francesco Pachì**, based in Italy, photographed the European knife collections. They traveled to where the collections were homed, coordinating these visits with the busy schedules of the collectors. Through the amazing images that they produced, I was granted the artistic freedom (and responsibilities) of a museum's curator and was able to display these treasures for the whole world to enjoy! And I did my best, exhibiting 650 of the most amazing modern custom knives, in one volume, combining them to show their beauty and designing each page for the highest visual impact, while also displaying various enlarged details of some of these incredible artistic knives.

There are many to whom I owe tremendously for helping me out during these fascinating years, and for doing everything so wholeheartedly to help me realize this goal. A goal that seemed important to them as it was for me and for the whole of the knife community, but also for the rest of the art-loving world.

I have to begin with **Phil Lobred** for inviting me to the 2001 AKI show in San Diego. This enabled me to present my original concept for the first book to a group of the most prominent knife artists in the world, giving a first breath of life to the fulfillment of a dream. And then, from that day on, constantly promoting my concepts for the additional volumes wherever and whenever he found appropriate.

Then there is my dear friend, **Don Guild**, a collector of art knives and a man of vast experience, whom I deeply thank for his continuous encouragement and down to earth advice, and for being there for me whenever I needed him.

Thanks are due to **Dr. Fred Carter** for finding the time to make for me the engraved set of 4 knives shown on the opening page of the preface. To **Owen Wood** and **Amayak Stepanyan** as well as **Howard Hitchmough** and **Tim George** for creating two fabulous folders especially for the book, and to **Edmund Davidson** for the *David Darom subhilt* he made for the preface.

Opposite page, from the left:
Dellana™, USA
"Melted Gold Pendant", 2003
The melted gold "Hamsa" (hand with five fingers, symbol of good luck) pendant was made for the collector's wife. It was created as a matching piece for the "Gold Rush" folder shown beside it. Length 1 7/8" (48 mm).
"Gold Rush", 1999
Lock back folder with a composite Damascus blade forged by Dellana with 14k yellow gold "Dellana Dots" as blade opening assist. Handles are presentation grade Mother-of-Pearl, inlaid with 14k gold dots and diamonds set in 14k yellow gold. Bolsters and lockbar "saddle" are fabricated of 14k yellow gold that is first fused, then formed and forged by hand (by Dellana) to create a unique "melted" look. These are different from side to side, due to the way the technique works. Liners are fileworked with the "Dentil" pattern. Spine of blade, lock bar and spring-keeper are inlaid with numerous tiny 14k yellow gold dots. All pins are 14k yellow gold.
Overall length 6" (152 mm).
"JOY", 2006
Lock back folder with a composite Damascus blade forged by Dellana with 14k yellow gold and ruby thumb stud fabricated by Dellana. Handles are presentation grade Mother-of-Pearl, inlaid with 24k gold dots and diamonds set in 14k yellow gold. Bolsters (front and rear) are 14k yellow gold engraved and textured. Liners are fileworked with "Dentil" pattern. Spine of blade, lock bar and spring-keeper are fileworked inside and out, with texturing on the lock release area. All pins are 14k yellow gold.
Overall length 6 1/8" (155 mm).

Above:
A knife collection can be stored and displayed in a large safe room, which allows viewing the entire collection very easily without having to engage in any direct handling. Shown here is part of the Gerald Hopkin collection.

Special thanks go to each and every one of the collectors who shared their exquisite possessions with all of us, and made this book a true world-class exhibition for the art of modern custom knives.

Special thanks also go to my dear friend **Paolo Saviolo**, the true gentleman and connoisseur of the arts, who believed in my vision and encouraged and backed me all the way. He took upon himself, with his unique Italian charm, the complicated job of printing this book and the difficult job of distributing all of my books all over the world as well as having them translated and whole editions printed in additional languages.

Opposite page, from the top:
Van Barnett, USA
"Wings", 2007
The blade is Van's W2 and 203-e Damascus. Carved Nickel Damascus wings, 14k gold bail and thumbstud and textured 14k gold shields on handle. Overall length 6 3/4" (171 mm).
"Gold and Lace", 2007
The blade is Van's W2 and 203-e Damascus. 14k gold engraved and textured front and rear bolsters. Lace pattern style Damascus handles. Overall length 6 3/4" (171 mm).

Both knives from the collection of Dr. Thad Kawakami-Wong, Hawaii.

Dr. David Darom, the author, and Paolo Saviolo, the publisher, introducing the third book in the series on modern custom knives at the 2006 BLADE Show in Atlanta.
Photo: Amayak Stepanyan

Opposite page:
Howard Hitcmough, USA
"Autumn Glory", USA
Made especially for the book, this round front liner lock folder has a 2 3/4" (70 mm) blade made from the Heimskringla pattern of Damasteel. The titanium liners are bead blasted and anodized a soft blue color. The back spacer is rope-worked stainless steel. The handle is made from heat-treated 416 stainless steel with engraving and 24k gold inlays by Tim George. The pivot collars are 18k gold as is the thumb-stud, which is set with a sapphire.
Overall length 6 1/2" (165 mm).

To **Nomi Morag**, world-class designer, who new how to put together everything I created and produce an amazing ready-for-print package.

Last but not least, my wife **Tehiya** and my children and grandchildren, who put up with my long "disappearing" acts in front of the computer for more than five years, while plunging totally into another world. **Nir** my son and **Naomi** his wife, designers 'par excellance', who checked and re-checked everything I did and helped me bring this production to the quality all of us can now be proud of.

Dr. David Darom
June 2007

The History of the Art Knife Invitational
Dr. David Darom

Opposite page, from the left:

William F. Moran, USA,

"Southwestern Bowie", 2003

Curly maple handle with silver wire inlay. Made for the 2003 AKI Show. Blade length 7" (178 mm). Owned by Phil Lobred, USA.

"Spear Point Bowie", 1993

50th anniversary knife with silver wrapped pommel and 23 silver studs. Made for the 1993 AKI Show. Blade length 9 1/2" (241 mm). Owned by Tommy Hutton, USA.

"ST-24", 1997

Curly maple handle with silver wire inlay. Made for the 1997 AKI Show. Blade length 12" (305 mm). Owned by Tommy Hutton, USA.

The idea for the Art Knife Invitational was that of longtime collector Phil Lobred. Until the formation of the Knifemakers Guild in 1970, networking among knifemakers was almost non-existent and certainly there were no "all knife" shows. In 1972, the "Knifemakers Guild Show" changed all that! Over the next ten years, other knife shows sprang up and custom knives gradually became more collectable. Still, the majority of custom knives being sold at knife shows were utility knives. But the knife market was evolving, and by 1980 there was definitely a move by a few collectors towards fancier, more embellished knives. The problem for the knifemaker was that to make such a knife was a risk of time, labor and material if there was no ready buyer. It seemed to Phil Lobred that the time was right for a new type of knife show. A show that would bring together the handful of knifemakers that wanted to create these "new" art knives and the handful of collectors that wanted to collect them.

I had attended several Cowboy Artists of America shows at the Phoenix Art Museum", said Lobred, "and I was impressed by two things. The name in the hat, draw concept and the voting in of new members by the existing members. I spoke with my old friends Ted and Betty Dowell about my idea, and they liked it and agreed to help with the details. At that point in time, the American art knife scene was in its infancy. The name 'art knife' was selected as the most descriptive, and 'invitational' seemed appropriate. So the Art Knife Invitational became a dream-come-true.

It was up to Lobred not only to select this first group of "art knife" makers but to convince them of the concept and solicit enough money from each to put on this new-style show. Since it had to be a class act, it became a very expensive proposition for the small group of knifemakers. The elegant MGM Grand Hotel in Reno was chosen as the venue and the first show was set for 28 May 1983. Twenty makers were selected and sixteen of them agreed to participate: Fred Carter, T.M. Dowell, Jim Ence, H.H. Frank, Royal Hanson, Jim Hardenbrook, Larry Hendricks, Billy Mace Imel, Kemal (Don Fogg & Murad Sayen), Ron Lake, Robert Lum, William F. Moran, James Schmidt, Herman Schneider, Dwight Towell, and Buster Warenski. A guest was the engraver, Lynton McKenzie.

The first show was a real nail-biter. There were 16 knifemakers and 68 knives in the fully catered ballroom, but when the doors opened, only 24 collectors walked in. Phil remembers that day:

By using their customer data base, the knifemakers had supplied the mailing list for the show. Everyone on this list was invited and there was no charge to attend. Even this first show was fully catered, both food and drink. When I opened the doors and there were only 24 people I thought, 'Wow! I threw the biggest knife party of the year and nobody came!'

But, the knives were amazing, and the 24 collectors bought almost every knife in the room.

Show rules allow each bidder only one bid per knife. During the first show, the only way we could check and make sure no one double-bid was to collect all the boxes, one for each knife, before the draw, take them to a back room and check their contents one by one. It went pretty fast except for Bill Moran's boxes, which were stuffed full. After checking, I handed all the boxes back to the makers, who were waiting to draw names, except for Moran's, because his boxes were so full, it was taking us time to check. Bill got nervous and said 'Phil I didn't get my boxes back!' I said, 'Well Bill, there was nothing in them so we just threw them away.' He was quiet for a moment then, very humbly, said, 'But, I saw some people put bids in.' Then I explained that I'd had to hire extra people to help because he had so many bids! He just grinned. Bill remained just as popular, from the first AKI Show until he retired after the 2003 show.

By sales standards, the show was a success, and the MGM Grand was booked for the 1984 show. There were some problems though. The show was pressure-packed, stressful and, being fully catered, was very expensive to produce - and the makers had to foot the bill. The makers also elected not to vote in new makers but instead to have Phil Lobred select them. This first group of makers had not jelled, and by 1984 the show lost Royal Hanson, Jim Hardenbrook, Larry Hendricks, Kemal, Ron Lake and Herman Schneider. Selected to replace these makers were Sid Birt, Dan Dagget, Tim Herman and C. Grey Taylor, for a total of 14 makers. Once again the show opened with 57 magnificent knives but with only a handful of collectors attending. But here again, same as in '83, almost every knife was sold.

Even though measured by sales these shows were successful, they were difficult to produce, expensive for the makers and very stressful; and morale was low because of the small attendance.

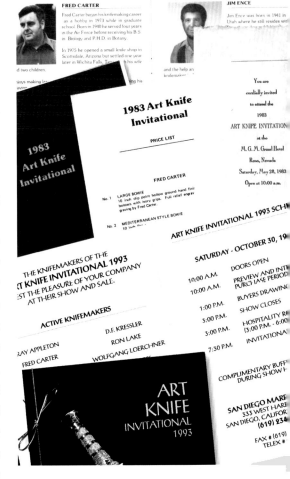

Above:
1983 AKI catalog, price list and invitation.
1993 AKI price list and catalog.

Above:

**1983 AKI Knifemakers
and Guest Engravers**

Back row, left to right: Larry Hendricks,
Ron Scaggs, Herman Schneider, Jim
Hardenbrook, Murad Sayen, Lynton
McKenzie, Dr. Fred Carter, Buster
Warenski, Dwight Towell and Bob Lum.
Front row, left to right: Ron Lake,
William F. Moran, Henry H. Frank, Ted
M. Dowell, Phil Lobred, James Schmidt,
Royal Hanson and Billy Mace Imel.

Lobred thought the commitment from the makers was not strong
enough and decided it was premature for the market to support
a knife show of this sort. He wrote the makers and told them
that he was going to put the show on hold until the knife market
grew stronger and the makers had more resolve for the concept
of a show of this type.

By 1990 the knife market was changing rapidly and "art
knives" were becoming more mainstream. At the 1991 Knifemakers
Guild Show, several makers approached Lobred about trying the
show once again. It was decided that it was in the makers' and
collectors' best interests to hold this show every other year.
Lobred agreed to pick the first 25 makers for the initial group
but insisted that from that point on, new members be voted in by
majority vote. Everyone agreed, and the next show was set for
30 October 1993 in San Diego, California. The only real change
in the structure of sales was the addition of the open-bid knife.
Each maker had the option to place one knife on open bid with
no reserve. 25 knifemakers were selected for this show, half from

Michael Walker, USA,
"Sharktooth Zipper", 1999
Composite blade of titanium and
stainless Damascus. Stainless
Damascus handle with gold, silver,
Meteorite, niobium and zirconium.
Made for the 1999 AKI Show. Blade
length 6" (152 mm). Owned by Ray
Sobieck, USA.

Pierre Reverdy, France,
"Integral Damascus Dagger", 2003
Enameled handle by Nicole Reverdy.
Made for the 2003 AKI Show.
Overall length 11" (279 mm).

T. M. Dowell, USA,
"Integral Hilt and Cap", 1997
Fossil walrus ivory handle. Oak leaf
and gold engraving by Julie Warenski.
Made for the 1997 AKI Show. Blade
length 6" (152 mm). Owned by Ray
Sobieck, USA.

the old guard and the other half new comers, with the emphasis on proven, collectable makers. Phil saw to every detail:

We kicked off the new 1993 show using Buster Warenski s King Tut dagger on the cover of both the invitation and the catalog. We also used the tag line, 'Now that s an art knife taken from the line by Paul Hogan in the movie Crocodile Dundee, 'Now that s a Knife!

This time the show attracted not only American collectors but also collectors from Europe and Japan. Once again, sales were excellent and the show came close to selling out. The next show in 1995, was on the drawing board, and the "Art Knife Invitational" was off and running.

If success is measured in sales, every Art Knife Invitational to date has been highly successful and has helped contribute to the establishment of the art knife as a unique art collectable. For Phil Lobred, success is measured in giving the makers the ability to be more creative so the collectors can reap the rewards.

Dave Nittinger, collector of high-end custom knives, writes about the AKI:

In the world of knife shows, there are shows and then there is the San Diego 'Art Knife Invitational. It occurs, of course, only every other year. When you come to San Diego for this show late in October, you will find great weather, a fantastic hotel, and great food. You will soon locate the best of the best with regard to knifemakers. In the year 2000, I suggested to Phil Lobred, our host, that we allow the collectors to bring some of their pieces that they would like to sell or trade and to display them after the show ended. After much conversation with the 25 makers they agreed to try it. After the 1p.m. drawing, and when all AKI business was done, the showroom was open to the collectors for about 3 hours for a buy, sell or trade session. It is a very popular time for many, and today it has added a great element to the venue. This also ensures that none of the collectors go home empty-handed. Yes, the show is only one day but the ambience is incredible. The ability to spend quality time with the makers is a great experience for everyone.

The Collector
Dave Nittinger, USA

**From the collection of
Dave Nittinger**

Dennis Friedly, *"Rose Bud Bowie", 2006*
Solvang Show, Best of Show knife.
Fossil walrus ivory, engraving by Gil
Rudolph, 24k gold and 416 stainless
fittings. Blade steel is 440C.
Overall length 14" (356 mm).

*"Each year the 65+ makers at the
Solvang Show (California, USA) pick
one knife that represents the best
of the best. The year was 2005 and I
purchased a Friedly Bowie. If that knife
had been entered for the "best of show"
award, my belief is that it would have
won. However, Dennis did not enter it
and that was that... I asked Dennis to
start a new project, to be finished in
time for next year's show. First came
the idea and then the work started.
The knife was completed literally hours
before the judging at the 2006 show.
There was with much anticipation
among the two hundred plus makers
and guests as they waited for Shelley
Berman to announce the winner. Their
roar could be heard for miles around
when Dennis Friedly's knife won best of
the show, as expected."*

Collecting guns was my hobby for many years until I discovered that no one ever met, spoke to or collaborated with Mr. Smith, Mr. Wesson or Mr. Colt. It was at this point that I attended my first knife show and right there is the reason for my involvement with this wonderful world of custom handmade knives. At these shows, the person standing across the table from you is the creator. It is easy to ask questions, to get answers, to learn and in time to collaborate with the maker to create the knife of your dreams.

My first "great show" was in Solvang (California), about 22 years ago. The first day consisted of walking around, trying to take in everything and not understanding much. On the second day I met Stan Hawkins who was a well-known collector of fine Warenski daggers and knives by Erickson, Ence and Rigney. He introduced me to Dennis Friedly, who became my first knife purchase. I also learned that Stan was a scrimshaw artist and had learned from Bob Engnath, who later became another friend. It was from this show that friendships with the makers started to grow and blossom. My longtime friend Don Hume was with me at this show, and he asked one maker how he had done something. Don produced a pad of paper and began drawing and writing out the procedure detailed by the maker. He later began making knives of his own and you can see one of his magnificent creations in the pages ahead.

These makers are glad to help you understand their world, and they will invite you to their shops, explaining along the way. It was a pleasure to meet Joe Cordova and visit his incredible shop. I watched as he forged a piece of steel that would later become one of my knives. I visited Michael and Pat Walker in Taos and watched as he worked with color titanium in their silly-looking oven at the time. It was great to spend hours with Bob Loveless in his shop, talking about anything and everything.

What you will see in this book are portions of some of the major modern custom knife collections from around the world. Many of the knives are the product of quiet conversations between the collector and the maker, sketching a new knife, which, in most cases, will be created, delivered and never seen by the public. We must thank these collectors for giving the makers that which is necessary to create this pure art. We must also thank the makers for the greatness that will be with us forever.

"The River That Carries Us"
Hilton Purvis, South Africa

Opposite page, from the left:

**From the collection of
Dr. John Anthony, UK**

Warren Osborne, 2005
Black-lip pearl interframe, engraved by Julie Warenski.
Overall length 6 1/2" (165 mm).

Warren Osborne, 2005
Folding dagger, with a Damascus blade by Mike Norris and Black-lip pearl scales. Engraved by Julie Warenski.
Overall length 6 1/2" (165 mm).

Tim Herman, 2000
Small coke-bottle folder interframe with carnelian agate. Engraved by Tim George.
Overall length 5 3/4" (146 mm).

Jack Busfield, 1989
Folding dagger Gold-lip pearl interframe with paua shell escutcheons. Engraved by the late Dan Wilkison.
Overall length 6" (152 mm).

"My interest has always been medium size folding knives, usually interframes. Although I have various Lakes and Walkers the last two years have seen the acquisition of decorated and engraved knives usually by Warren Osborne, Tim Herman and Steve Hoel. My favourite engravers are Julie Warenski, Tim George, Jon Robyn and Dan Wilkison".

My grandfather used to play a game with me when I was a child, asking "which came first, the chicken or the egg, the egg or the chicken?". It was always great fun, and as I got older my answers to his question would get more logical and reasoned, but we never solved the riddle. The riddle holds true for our craft of handmade knives and poses the question, which came first, the knife makers and their knives, or the collectors and their collections? We could probably devote the entire chapter to this question, but I am not sure if I want to reach an answer. I prefer to leave it unresolved and enjoy the give and take, request and delivery, temptation and succumbing relationship that exists between knife makers and their collectors.

I recall some years ago having dinner with one of our Guild members, a naturally skilled craftsman with magic in his fingers. Present that evening was a new friend, a successful businessman, someone skilled in the art of balance sheets, but not with his hands. This man was dumbfounded when he learned that most of the furniture in the room had been made by the host. He walked around the house, touching the chairs, the tables, the fireplace, the display cabinets, all the time asking "did you make this?" and "what about this?". In his world you purchased the items you needed, you did not make them yourself. For a knifemaker and knife collector market to exist, there have to be those who can make, and those who can buy.

At some point a random assembly of knifemakers realized that they could muster sufficient interest from their equally loose number of buyers to warrant organizing a small exhibition. Buyers in turn saw that others shared their interest, and together they had enough knives to justify calling themselves collectors. The exhibitions attracted more new makers, and buyers. When this had gained a certain momentum it needed to be harnessed, organized and formalized, and thus Guilds came into being. The Guilds gave the makers more credibility, and the collectors more confidence.

In the 1970's this coming together of like minds in the pursuit of handmade knives had a certain survivalist edge to it, a desperation to bond with others in what was a lonely knife making landscape. The pioneer makers needed to be self-motivated and self-sufficient for they were thin on the ground with little or no supporting infrastructure. There is a dynamic involved in the custom knife making industry, not just the interaction between knife maker and knife buyer, but also in the manner in which the craft moves and travels around them, like a current sweeping them along a lazy river. The river is occupied by more than the two main parties being discussed as we also have casual buyers, dealers, suppliers, shops, clubs, guilds and shows. All are being carried along with the same shared interest of knife making, albeit in different ways. No craft can operate in a vacuum, and in an environment where there is sufficient interest a network will develop which will eventually become self-perpetuating. Thirty years later that landscape is considerably more inviting. Supplies and suppliers abound, knowledge is available through any number of courses, books, videos, DVDs and the Internet. Product can be bought and sold privately, through dealers, shows, or Internet websites. It almost looks easy. Almost.

The future of our craft is no longer tentative, its existence is guaranteed. However the early knife maker challenges of actually practicing the craft have been replaced by the challenge of widespread competition. Whether the collector suffers any differently or experiences increased pressure is debatable. Certainly their own pond has considerably more fish in it, but they are also spoiled for choice. The early days of clubs, guilds and shows were focused on learning and development. These days it is more about showing and sharing. There can be no doubt that the interaction between knife makers and collectors has pushed both parties to new heights of excellence and demand. The current status of modern scrimshaw owes a great deal to knife making which was a carrier for a wave of new artists twenty years ago. The advances made in the practical and decorative use of titanium come to mind, as do the number of folding knife locking mechanisms, varieties of modern blade steels, and huge strides made in the forging of pattern Damascus. Add to this custom knifemaking's unique ability to balance practical and high end art, folding and fixed, budget and expensive.

All of these factors combine in our ever-flowing river to keep the craft alive and will carry it through to future generations. For as long as it does so we can be assured that wonderfully skilled crafts persons will be discovered, and great collections will continue to be assembled.

Opposite page, from the left:
From the collection of Cheryl Dibley, UK

Owen Wood, USA
"Art-Deco Liner Lock", 2004
Engraved scales, fluted Damasteel bolster, blued 303 stainless steel back spacer with eleven diamond chips. Engraved by Tim George.
Overall length 4 5/8" (117 mm).
"Art-Deco Liner Lock", 2003
Blued 303 stainless steel, Mother-of-Pearl and Black-lip pearl.
Overall length 5 11/16" (145 mm).
Warren Osborne, USA
"Interframe Lockback", 2003
Mother-of-Pearl, rose gold. Engraved by Julie Warenski, Mike Norris Damascus.
Overall length 5 1/2" (140 mm).
Kaj Embretsen, Sweden
"3 Blade Slip-Joint Warncliff Wittler", 2001
Mother-of-Pearl and gold pins, Embretsen's Snowflake pattern Mosaic Damascus bolsters and Twist pattern Damascus blade.
Overall length 7 1/2" (191 mm).
Larry Fuegen, USA
"Lockback Revival Folder", 1997
Carved MOP, Blued steel, 14k yellow gold liners and Fuegen Ladder pattern Damascus blade.
Overall length 6 1/2" (165 mm).

"Whilst my initial interest was inspired by fixed blade knives I quickly moved to collecting small to medium sized folding knives, fascinated by their size and opening mechanisms. I have an eclectic taste and require only that an individual piece has a quality that sets it apart; an intrinsic beauty which means the knife has an immediate appeal. This appeal relates centrally to the integrity of the design, the subtle and complimentary use of materials and engraving and finally the quality of execution and attention to detail"

Marlene's Small-Scale Masterpieces
Dr. David Darom

Marlene Marton began her unique collection of small knives as a direct outcome of her desire to support her husband's nascent interest in knives. For years her husband, whose collection is featured elsewhere in this book, was attracted to knives at various craft shows, but he never indulged his interest. One year Marlene decided to purchase a knife for his birthday. Off she went to the San Francisco Gun Exchange, where she viewed the available knives. They were a bit more expensive then she had imagined, so she decided that having her husband with her to make the choice was the way to go. When both returned, they had the pleasure of meeting Nate Posner, the owner. Nate was a wonderful man and a major supporter of many knifemakers. After several hours of viewing and education, they were surprised when Nate decided that he would not sell them the knife they had chosen. He felt that with their interest in knifemaking they should attend a show, meet the knifemakers, and support them directly. The first Solvang show (1985) was about to take place, and Nate provided the information they needed to attend. As an aside, the Knifemaker's Guild began awarding the "Nate Posner Award" annually after he passed away.

The Solvang show did indeed initiate their overall collection, although Marlene's own unique focus would follow a few years later. In truth, Marlene was not a true knife lover; quite the contrary, knives conjured up uncomfortable thoughts of her upbringing on the Lower East Side of New York where knives had utilities other than collecting. Over time, she became increasingly comfortable with knives, appreciating the skills necessary to craft them and the artistic results. She decided that she would collect knives, mostly folders, which were approximately 3 1/2" in overall length, although a few exceptions exist.

The challenge then began, as this was not the type of knife routinely being crafted by knifemakers. The question was how to encourage them to utilize their abilities to create a true representation of their skills in this smaller format? It turned out to be somewhat difficult, as Marlene wanted knives from the best of the best, and these were busy folks not looking for new challenges. Her persistence, and her personal friendships with the knifemakers eventually won out, and stunning small knives were made for her.

While each knife has a special story that goes with it, one of

Marlene Marton's Small Scale Fixed Blades

Joel Osmond, USA, *2005*
Mintubi Australian crystal opal blade, opal fluorite (Tiffany Stone) handle. Overall length 3 3/8" (86 mm).
Jim Kelso, USA
"Ice Crystal", 1992
Dagger, Phillip Baldwin Damascus blade, cast and engraved sterling handle with enameled silver inlay. Ebony sheath.
Overall length 3 3/8" (86mm).
Johnny Walker Nilsson, Sweden
"Marlene", 2005
Swedish Sami, Nilsson Damascus blade, engraved reindeer antler. Carved and engraved reindeer sheath. Overall length 4" (102 mm).
Don Fogg and Murad Sayen, USA
"Tudorfish", 1993
Dagger, carved Damascus blade, blued and textured steel, carved fossilized walrus ivory and opal inlayed handle. Overall length 3 1/2" (89 mm).

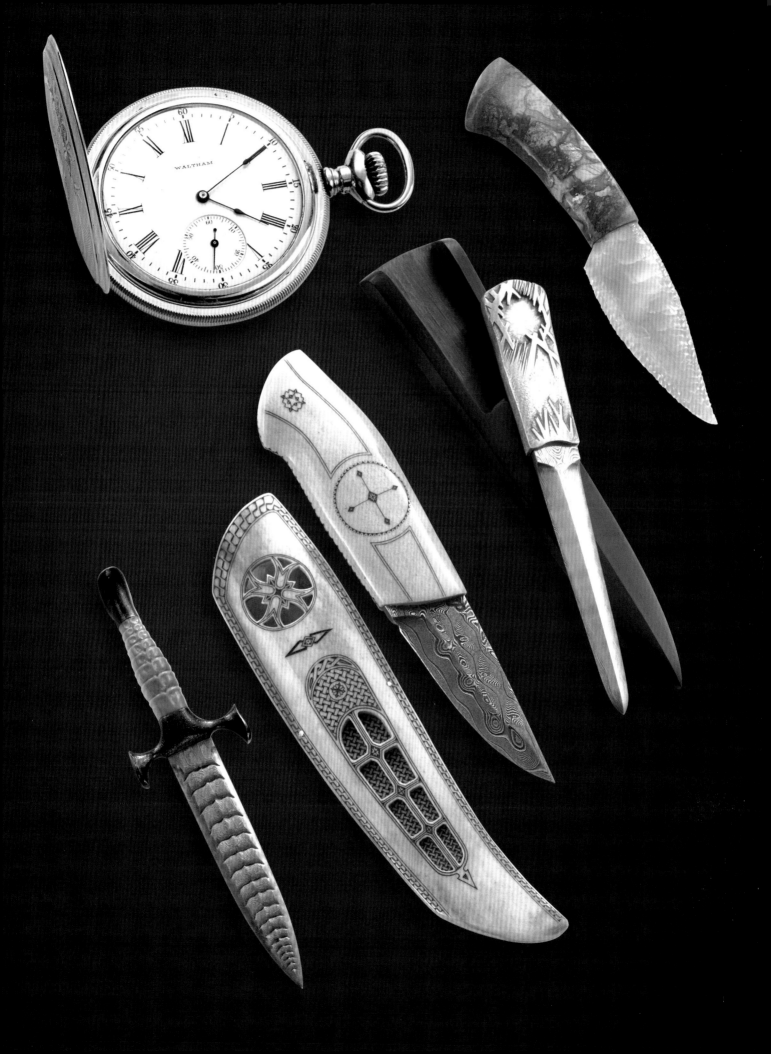

the knives shown in this chapter is the smallest folder ever made by the incredible Jim Schmidt. For years Jim insisted that he could not make such a small knife. However, one day Jim handed Marlene an exquisite knife made to his exacting specifications, just in reduced size. When asked how much the knife would cost, he said, *"You see these hands? They're too big to make a knife that small. If you can't make it, you can't charge for it"*. A wonderful gift, from a wonderful man!

Other knives that belong to Marlene's collection have already been included in earlier volumes of my books, and larger knives by Virgil England, Henry Frank, Michael Walker, and Ray Appleton are shown in her husband's chapter of this book. In fact, both Marlene and Larry share their collections and their lives completely.

Opposite page, left to right and top to bottom:

Marlene Marton s Small Scale Folding knives

Gary Blanchard, *"Zebra" 2002, Folder*
440C etched blade, anodized titanium handle with engraving and ceramic resin artwork, button lock. Overall length 4 3/4" (121 mm).

Van Barnett, *"Mini-Raven", 1999*
Liner lock, Damascus blade, carved and textured blued steel handle, gold. Overall length 3" (76 mm)

Josh Smith, *Liner lock, 2006*
Damascus blade and bolsters, carved Black-lip pearl handle. Overall length 3 1/2 (89 mm).

Warren Osborne, *1994*
Interframe lock back, green sea snail inlays, ATS-34 blade, engraved by Lynton McKensie. Overall length 3 1/4" (83 mm).

Kaj Embretsen, *2004*
Two-bladed sway back slip joint, Damascus blades, gold and Black-lip pearl handle, engraved by Julie Warenski. Overall Length 3 3/4" (95 mm).

Dellana, *"Starfire", 1999*
Lock back, composite Damascus blade, gold and Black-lip pearl handle. Overall length 3 1/2" (89 mm).

Warren Osborne, *1994*
Interframe lock back, Black-lip pearl inlays, ATS-34 blade, engraved by Steve Lindsay. Overall length 3 1/2" (89 mm).

Shane Taylor, *"Diamond", 2003*
Liner lock, Mosaic Damascus blade and handle, carved mammoth ivory. Overall length 3 3/4" (95 mm).

Dellana, *"Baby Beauty", 1996*
Lock back, San Mai Damascus blade, Sterling and Gold-lip pearl handle, gold and peridot. Overall length 3 1/2" (89 mm).

Robert Sidelinger, *1998,* Auto, Damascus blade, mokume and Black-lip pearl handle, ruby. Overall length 3 5/8" (92 mm).

Barry Davis, *2003,* Two-bladed Warncliff lock back, Damascus blades, gold liners, checkered and gold piquet Mother-of-Pearl handle. Overall length 4 7/8" (124 mm).

Charly Bennica, *2002,* Rear lock back interframe, Hank Knickmayer Damascus blade, red coral inlays. Overall length 4" (102 mm).

Fred Carter, *1991,* Mini folding dagger lock back. Blued steel blade and handle, gold and silver inlays. Overall length 3" (76 mm).

Matthew Lerch, *"Lexington", 2004,* Mini auto button lock, Damascus blade, stainless and Black-lip pearl handle, engraved by Julie Warenski. Overall length 3 1/2" (89 mm).

James Schmidt, *"Sweet Pea"* (late 1980 s early 1990 s). Lock back, Damascus blade and bolsters, Gold-lip pearl. Overall length 3 1/2" (89 mm).

Rick Eaton, *2000,* Side lock step down folder, 440C blade, 416SS handle with carving, engraving and pearl inlays. Overall length 3 9/16" (91 mm).

Ron Newton, *"Angel Wing", 1999,* Liner lock, Mosaic gold-plated Damascus blade and bolsters, Gold-lip pearl. Overall length 3 1/2" (89 mm).

Buster Warenski, *1992,* Persian lock back, 440C blade, gold handle with fire opal inlays. Overall length 3" (76 mm).

Owen Wood, *2005,* Art Deco liner lock, composite Damascus blade, gold bolsters, MOP and Black-lip pearl, engraved by Amayak Stepanyan. Overall length 3" (76 mm).

Tim Herman, *"Mini-Sliver", 2005,* Slip joint, ATS-34 blade, 416SS handle, color engraved. Overall length 4 1/2" (114 mm).

Michael Walker, *1988,* Liner lock, stainless blade, niobium handle, engraved by Patricia Walker. Overall length 2 1/8" (54 mm).

Robert Weinstock, *2001,* Lock back, Damascus blade and handle, carved and chased, gold. Overall length 3 5/8" (92 mm).

Howard Hitchmough, *"Ariel", 2000,* Lock back, stainless Damascus blade and handle, gold liners. Overall length 3 1/2" (89 mm).

The Dress Tactical Folding Knife
Neil Ostroff, Canada

I recall vividly the first time that I met David Darom. It was in New York City at the 2003 ECCKS (East Coast Custom Knife Show). He was there as an exhibitor to promote his book, *Art and Design in Modern Custom Folding Knives*, the first in what was destined to be a series of definitive reference books in the fascinating world of custom knives. I purchased two books and asked him to inscribe each of them. After signing the title page of the first one for me, I asked him to dedicate the second one to my parents. He asked me if they were interested in knives. "No", I explained, "I want them to have something to put on their coffee table so that when their friends come over and ask, yet again, what their son Neil does for a living they will have something to show them!"

Other than knife collectors, few people understand the rationale of purchasing something as *ordinary* as a knife for hundreds, often thousands, of dollars. Yet to those who do - the rationale is *rational.*

This section, *The Dress Tactical Folding Knife*, is the insightful journey towards the furthest and most creative horizon the custom knifemaker attempts to explore. It is a place, always in view yet always in the distance, where he or she can let the imagination roam unchallenged and unbridled.

This is not just physical labor; this is a passionate love affair of meticulous detail, which focuses attention on the most incomprehensible levels of craftsmanship from which is borne a final product worthy of being displayed in a museum or treasured under the glass of a showcase in a billionaire's palatial mansion.

Every knife, even these works of art, is still a fully functional tool and can always do the job it was designed to do - to cut. Some of us can achieve satisfaction just by carrying these mechanical marvels in our pockets like our own little magic stone or talisman that only we can understand and appreciate. Others still see them only as tools and simply use them - and use them hard. For all, to possess a beautiful knife, like the examples you see on these pages, is simply pride of ownership taken to the highest level.

Over the last ten years, the market and appetite for these edged treasures has seen some of the most dramatic growth in the knife industry. Moreover, there are no signs of this fascination waning.

A knifemaker, who may have been, just a few years ago, one

Opposite page, from the top:
Ken Onion, Hawaii
"DeadSexy", 2006
Blade steel is 154V. Titanium handle with burgundy micarta coral pattern inlay. Speed Safe assisted opening. Overall length 8 3/4" (222 mm).
"Timascus Tirade", 2005
Cowry steel blade. Acid washed and selectively heat-colored Timascus handle with Mother-of-Pearl inlays and Speed Safe assisted opening. Overall length 9 1/4" (235 mm).
"Taboo", 2006
Mike Norris stainless Random pattern Damascus blade steel. Holstein cow pattern inlayed in a 6al4v frame lock titanium handle. Speed Safe assisted opening.
Overall length 8 1/8" (206 mm).
"Zero Tolerance Prototype", 2006
Mike Norris Random pattern Damascus blade steel. Anodized titanium handle with bark mammoth inlays. Speed Safe assisted opening. Overall length 8 3/4" (222 mm).

of the hottest and most desirable bladesmiths in the arena, is now being challenged from all directions as new and younger players are coming onto the scene on a regular basis. In addition, several of the veterans have resurfaced to give these youngsters a run for their money. But in the end, only a select few will reach the incredible level of talent, success, and perhaps notoriety as those iconic makers that you see represented in these pages.

So here we are. We have taken the knife, the most primitive and basic tool of man, and pushed and dragged it through sheer effort and dedication towards the pinnacle of mechanical and artistic achievement of human capability. And yet, the most frequent collectors of these works of art are still just ordinary human beings who have developed and nurtured an unexplainable fascination for these bladed implements. Even the most prolific and knowledgeable collector is often at a loss for words to explain exactly why we seek out and treasure these often misunderstood collectibles. This book is a bridge to that understanding.

This article illustrates one growing field in the world of custom knives. It provides a glimpse at the dramatic form, design and materials used today to create *Upscale Tactical Knives,* or *Dress Tacticals* as many refer to them. The choices were many but the space was limited. I do hope that the following words by some of the prominent custom tactical knifemakers and examples of their most recent work (some of it made specially for the book), speak for themselves.

Opposite page, from the left:
Darrel Ralph, USA
Dress "Gun Hammer RADIAN", 2006
Integral side bar lock. Flat ground Mike Norris stainless Ladder pattern Damascus modified recurve Tanto blade in an exclusive RADIAN design. Gripper grooves at strategic points along the frame. Carved and contoured solid Mike Norris stainless Gator Skin Damascus handle with Picasso marble inlays. Tritium inserts in the frame. Frame is 3D contoured (not flat) to fit the hand. Overall Length 8 3/4" (mm). Weight 5.9 ounces (165 grams).

Greg Lightfoot, Canada
Dress "Catch Dog", 2006
Upscale Tactical Liner Lock Folder. Megalodon Tooth pattern Damasteel blade and bolsters. Bead blasted titanium frame and liners with triple thongholes. Serrated thumb ramp on the frame. Canadian Yukon mastodon ivory scales. Stainless steel thumbstud with hematite inlay. Long false-edge top on front. Mastodon ivory backspacer posts. Heat colored screws and pivot.
Overall length 9" (229 mm). Weight 6.2 ounces (173 grams).

Darrel Ralph, USA
"When I began making knives in the late 1980's", he explains, "The market was dominated by high-end art Interframe folders. This also was the beginning of the refined switchblade-knife era. By the time the decade was out, the focus had shifted to more Spartan, pure tactical knives with bare-knuckled brawling styles and designs. Though I was an established high-art folder and switchblade maker by that time, I saw this paradigm shift as an opportunity to create the ideal "Man's Knife" by blending the essential elements of style and function into what others and I call the Dress Tactical Folder. Carrying a knife is a masculine habit that meets man's need for tools to modify his environment - what I call the technician factor. Dress tactical knives connect man's technician factor to one of his strongest urges: to impress others with his lifestyle. The best dress tactical folders are the synthesis of artfully styled knives with true high-performance form and function".

Darrel Ralph uses the best steel available for his blades. His ultimate choices being S30V, Stellite 6K and Mike Norris stainless Damascus. He is currently working with specialty steel producers to develop a new alloy that may outperform anything used so far. Darrel focuses on function, precision and high quality in all the knives he produces.

Ken Onion, Hawaii

"I truly love knives and have, according to my parents, admired them from the age of 3. I collected knives before I started making them myself in 1991. Stan Fujisaka taught me, and I have never slowed down ever since. I really enjoy pushing my own limits and exploring new concepts. The only thing more satisfying than seeing a customer truly love a knife he or she are handling, would be to watch a new young knifemaker you are mentoring or have inspired, evolve into a skilled craftsman. I continually strive to create very special custom knives that the owners could not only claim as their favorite carry pieces, but to be also used and appreciated for more than just their appearance".

Ken teaches knifemaking, folder making and gives advanced classes to new makers, as well as experienced knifemakers. He also teaches designing classes as well as business theory and strategy. Over the years he has made knives for numerous celebrities and in 1998 signed on with Kershaw Knives as their designer, winning two American Made Knife of the Year awards and an European Knife of the Year award. With over 35 patents, Ken's knives are primarily sporting designs, Zero Tolerance knives, military, police, EMT and high-end kitchen knives. His knives combine maximum mass with maximum performance as well as being as easy to use as possible. His designs are constantly evolving influenced by Fibronaci's principles of the natural flow and design in nature.

Greg Lightfoot, Canada

"When most customers talk to me about making a tactical knife, the conversation usually doesn't advance much beyond specifications like G-10 or carbon fiber handles and BG-42 or 20CV blades. One of my pure tacticals might start with a BG-42 satin finished modified Tanto blade and black G-10 scales and have a basic titanium pocket clip. A few might want to upgrade a little bit further to, say, Fibermascus scales with silver G-10 bolsters and a cool sheath. Just as tactical and utilitarian but the presentation is a bit fancier.

Then there are the collectors who are looking for something extra special, what I call an Upscale Tactical. They are usually people who already own some of my knives, know what to expect as far as construction and fit and finish go, and now want something with a bit more pizzazz! For a knife request like that, I might use Damascus for the blade, meteorite for the bolsters, and presentation-grade pearl for the handles. For these projects, I have also used fancy woods like ironwood burl, Canadian maple and others. A beautiful piece of stag or Canadian elk horn also produces great "dress" scales. Finally, the finest Yukon mammoth ivory and fossil walrus tusk are always a stunning compliment to my upscale knives. The pocket clip and the screw heads can be fileworked with fancy patterns, as can the spine of the blade or the spacer in a folder. Often, Damascus is used.

To me, upscale means more high-end materials and more time spent on embellishments. But, the function is the same, no matter how much one will spend on one of my knives.

In my opinion, a tactical/utility knife will always be a user knife first – whether it's an EDC (Every Day Carry) with G-10 scales or a special occasion full blown upscale piece with a Damascus blade, cool bolsters,

Opposite page from the top:

Pat and Wes Crawford, USA
"Special Triumph", 2006
"Dress Quick Draw" double bolster liner lock folder, with a 4" (102 mm) Damasteel Recurve blade. Ancient fossil surface mammoth tusk scales. Double serrated guards. Blue anodized fileworked titanium liners. Double Damasteel bolsters. 6 sapphires and 2 cubic zirconium inset into the bolsters. Fully fileworked stainless backspacer. Layer of red micarta between the scales and liners. Stainless jeweled fileworked pocket clip. Spyderhole blade opener. Overall length 9 1/4" (235 mm). Weight 9.9 ounces (277 grams).

Mick Strider, USA
Custom "RC Nightmare Frame Lock", 2006
Jim Ferguson Damascus spear-point recurve NIGHTMARE grind blade (3/16" thick). Solid blast "Heat Striped" titanium frame-lock design with inset grooved black G10 scales. Oversized pivot. Dual titanium thumb studs with tritium. Indexing lock scallop. Heat striped solid titanium back bar. Serrated thumb ramps on the top of the frame and on the top of the blade. Bead blasted removable titanium pocket clip - tip up carry. Overall Length 9" (229 mm). Weight 9.2 ounces (250 grams).

Phil Boguszewski, USA
Dress "Piranha Flipper", 2006
Devin Thomas stainless steel Vines & Roses Damascus blade. Devin Thomas stainless steel Reptilian Damascus bolster. Premium giraffe anklebone scales. Anodized titanium liners. Titanium thumbstud with ruby. Fileworked thumb ramp and titanium back strap. Overall Length 8" (mm). Weight 5.4 ounces (151 grams).

and premium grade handles. No matter how much you "fancy" them up, deep down all of my knives start life as a tactical/utility – built hard-core to do the job".

"Lightfoot Knives" is located in the heart of Alberta, Canada, on 160 acres of untamed land. This is where Greg lives, works, hunts, raises game and most of all develops and tests every knife he designs. Greg's motto "innovation not imitation" has been the key in his 18 years as a knifemaker.

Mick Strider, USA

With few exceptions, Mick builds knives, with one thought in mind: A life could depend on the quality of this tool. For this reason he tends to lean towards a simplicity of design and overkill of construction mindset. Regardless of whether the knife will head "down range", or spend its life in a climate controlled safe, it always starts with the same, space-age materials and high-tech methods of manufacture.

"I am an incredibly lucky knife maker. Lucky in that my design intent often spills to both sides of the spectrum. My "Nightmare" grind is a prime example. The design intent is to remove weight while optimizing both cutting ability as well as tip strength. The "trisula" grind on the back of many of my folders, adds 'edge' without making the blade "double edged". While rather obtuse, the grind serves quite well as a scraping tool. Many find it useful for tasks such as scraping a gasket or magnesium fire starter... without the worry of damaging the primary cutting edge. Regardless of my intent while producing these grinds, the end result is a dramatic looking blade grind, which catches the attention of both users as well as collectors.

My tastes run a little more towards the archaic and antique, therefore I often try to create this look using modern materials. Not so much period type work, but period type feel. Because of this, I am not much of a coatings or anodizing guy. I tend to create my "style" with texture and heat. An example of this would be the stippling and heat coloring I apply to titanium. My goal is to create a tool that is not only as nearly perfect as I can make it functionally, but to add richness and hue that are nearly impossible to comprehend without actually holding the item in your hand. In the end, every knife is created to be used. Some are made for hard use, some are gentle and delicate... but in the feel of the cut, lies the true beauty of any blade".

Pat and Wes Crawford, USA

From the very beginning, in 1972, Pat Crawford loved to make fancy knives. He made fancy Fighters and Bowies. As time went on, he found a following of customers who had a need for a hard use self-defense knife, which is what he has been making for many years. As the eighties came to a close Pat and many other knifemakers were also making tactical folding knives. However, as these were in great demand, he did not devote enough time to the art knives, although he did continue to make a few fancier collector knives on occasion.

"My son, Wes Crawford started making knives full time in 1990. In 1999, he began taking on more of the finish work on the fancier folders. We both still do everything, but now he does more shop work and I am doing more design, office work, and try to keep him supplied

Opposite page, from the left:
Todd Begg, USA
"Megaladon", 2006
This flipper is the first one of its kind made by Todd. The Lock is what he calls an "integrated lock". It is a bolt-on-frame lock, a separate component thicker than the liners. The lock and liners are 6al4v titanium and the handle is stabilized curly koa wood. The inlay over the pivot is "lightning strike" carbon fiber. Blade steel is 154CM and the back spacer, made of S30V, has serrations for control in the reverse grip.
Overall length 11" (279 mm).
"Predator", 2005
Made of D2 tool steel, this knife is a Full Integral with Todd s In-Line handle style. The handle is made of stabilized curly koa wood. Megalodon (above) was made to create a matching pair with this knife. Blade length is 6" (152 mm) and the overall length 11" (279 mm).
"Glimpse", 2006
A flipper liner lock. The handle frame is G-10 and the inlays are red palm wood. Blade steel is 154CM. The liner and lock are 6al4v titanium as is the pocket clip. "The fine tuning of the flipper action I use is a technique I learned from Phil Boguzewski".
Overall length 8 7/8" (225 mm).
All three knives use threaded steel post construction for the screws.

All three knives from the collection of William J. Jury III, Alaska

with rough parts. He and I have always enjoyed making the higher quality upscale tactical folders and we continuously strive to find new ways to decorate them, while keeping keep the basic and simple lines of a truly functional folding knife. Making a variety of knives helps keep us creative and interested in our work, and these upscale knives gives us a new challenge that keeps us sharp and in tune with the demands of the demanding enthusiast. We are proud of all the knives we make, but showing off these fancy tactical folders is a real thrill".

Phil Boguszewski, USA

"It is my observation that upscale tactical folders have evolved with the tastes of the buyers. Knife publications and the wealth of information on the Internet have created a sophisticated and demanding public. Collectors are well versed in construction methods and material options, and looking at the total package. I believe that important factors in a good folding knife are: solid, trouble free construction, exacting fits and smooth motion, and a keen blade. When combined with exotic materials, the results are a useful tool, a thing of beauty, and a satisfying possession. Sometimes I wonder how blessed I am to be in a business where I get to spend time creating things of beauty that give pleasure to others. I'm proud that my long involvement in the handmade knife community has allowed me contribute to the body of very fine work done by many talented makers".

Phil Bobuszewski has been making all kinds of knives for many years. However, making the upscale tactical folding knives that were becoming so popular over these past few years are a thrill for him to make.

Todd Begg, USA

Todd developed an appreciation for fine knives deep forests of the Pacific Northwest, camping, hunting and trapping. He tried making a few knives while still in high school, in metal shop classes, and realized that it was not just a passing hobby, he had found his passion. Later, in the Army, he earned an associate degree in Machine Shop Technology, knowing that machining skills would help in his knife making abilities. Todd went full time with his knife making in 2003. Influenced by the amazing grinding skills of Bob Lum and Bill Luckette and the Integral construction of Edmund Davidson and Ted Dowell's knives, Todd developed what he calls his "In-line Handle".

"There has definitely been a new 'genre' of knives becoming known as Custom Tactical, Cadillac Tactical or Gentleman's Tactical", explains Todd. *"These tactical are like a Hummer, a pricey off road vehicle, with plush leather interiors, fine mahogany dashes and all the newest gadgetry but still capable of serious driving and tough use. I have pursued this type of model and style in my knives as it really inspires and appeals to me on a personal level. The majority of my knives are considered to be in this category of knives and the demand for the Gentleman's Tactical is voracious at this time".*

Opposite page, from the top:
Darrel Ralph, USA
"Madd Maxx 3 inch", 2006
Assisted opening folding dagger with an all stainless steel Mosaic Damascus blade and frame. The inlay is mammoth tooth.
Overall length 6 5/8" (168 mm).

"Madd Maxx 3 inch", 2006
Assisted opening folder with a titanium frame and a 3" (76 mm) S30v full ground dagger style blade. The inlay is Mother-of-Pearl with a Black-lip pearl inlay inside of that and two gold pins.
Overall length 6 5/8" (168 mm).

"Madd Maxx 3 inch", 2006
Assisted opening folder with a titanium frame and a 3" (76 mm) S30v Bowie style blade. The inlay is shaduko bone-yard.
Overall length 6 5/8" (168 mm).

"Madd Maxx 3 inch", 2006
Assisted opening folder with a titanium frame and a 3" (76 mm) S30v spear-point style blade. The inlay is shaduko spider web.
Overall length 6 5/8" (168 mm).

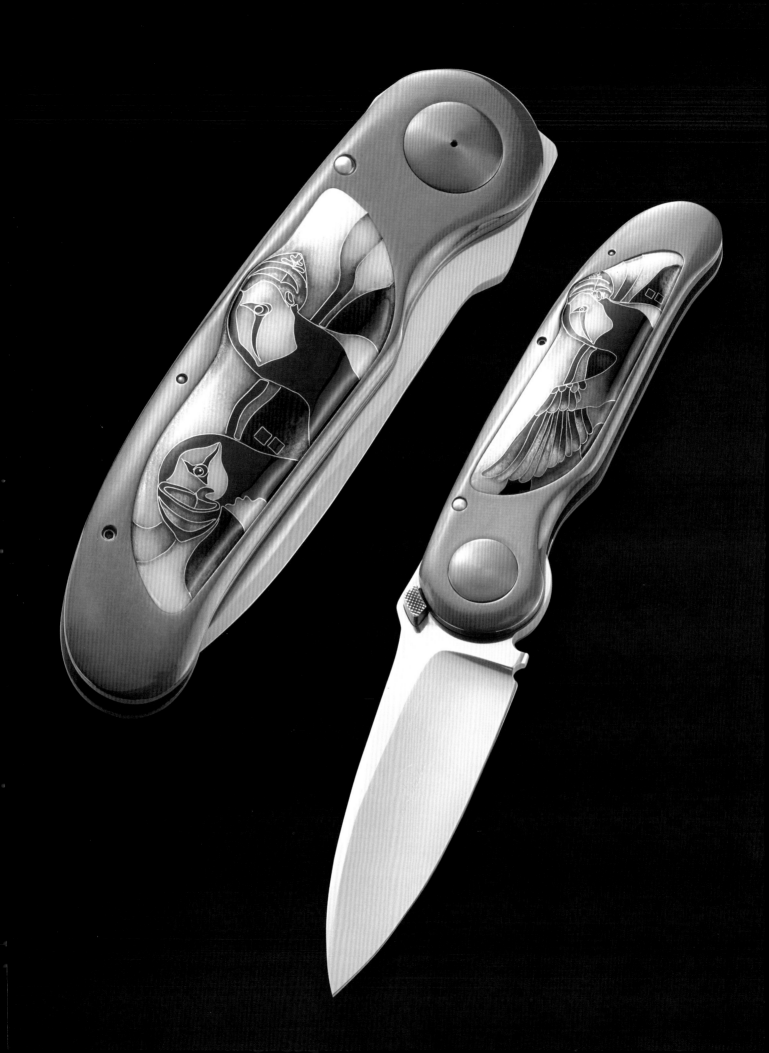

Dr. David A. Cohen

Dave Ellis

Jeff Gale

Don Guild

Tom and Gwen Guinn

Don Henderson

Walter Hoffman

Gerald Hopkin

Tommy C. Hutton

William J. Jury and William J. Jury III

Phil Lobred

Dr. Laurence J. Marton

Dave Nittinger

Luigi Peppini

Dr. Pierluigi Peroni

Wolf Schulz-Tattenpach

Ron Stagnari

Edward Stitt

Ed Wormser

Opposite page:
**Michael Walker and
Merry Lee Rae, USA**
"Puffin", 1993
Blade-lock folder, stainless steel
blade, anodized titanium handle with
cloisonné inlays (Rae). Overall length 7
5/8" (194 mm).
*"The fusion of these two marvelous
talents did not yield immediate
results. Merging the free flowing
art of cloisonné and the exacting
talents of an individual who deals
in thousands of an inch took time,
patience, and the creation of new
techniques. The results speak for
themselves"!*

From the collection of Dr. Laurence
Marton, USA

Opposite page, from the left:

Charly Bennica, France

"Caraïbe", 2005

Tail lock interframe folder in natural red coral. Blade is ATS-34, the handle is 416 stainless steel. Underwater scenes engraved by Ray Cover Jr. Overall length 6 3/4" (171 mm).

"Castor and Polux" Fixed-Blade, 2003

Fixed blade interframe in Mother-of-Pearl. Blade is ATS-34, the handle is 416 stainless steel.
Zebra scrimshaw by Francesco Amatori, engraving and gold inlays by Decorative Art.
Overall length 7 1/2" (190 mm).

"Castor and Polux" Folder, 2003

Tail lock interframe in Mother-of-Pearl. Blade is ATS-34, the handle is 416 stainless steel. Zebra scrimshaw by Francesco Amatori, engraving and gold inlays by Decorative Art.
Overall length 7 1/2" (190 mm).

"Egée", 2005

Tail lock interframe folder in natural red coral. Blade is ATS 34, the handle is 416 stainless steel.
Mermaid and octopus scenes engraved by Manrico Torcoli.
Overall length 6 3/4" (171 mm).

Dr. David Cohen USA

I was born in Chicago in 1956 and have been a practicing veterinarian since 1981. My passion for knife collecting began in 2003. I was surfing the internet looking to buy a gift for my jiu jitsu sensei. I came upon a beautiful gentleman's folder made with mammoth ivory and Damascus steel. I was intrigued by the duality of art and craftsmanship. I became hooked! My tastes have since "matured", and I have focused my attention on collecting folding knives that represent my love of animals and nature. I especially enjoy my knives engraved or scrimshawed with animals, birds and fish. I covet the pearls, corals and ivories that nature has created. I try to collect unique knives that can be instantly recognized as to which artist created them. The friendships that I have with many knife makers have made collecting that much more rewarding. To be involved in the project, and to have a relationship with the artist, brings great satisfaction. I am honored and flattered to be included among so many great collectors in this book.

Left, from the top:
Francesco Pachì, Italy
"Folding Utility", 2003
Liner lock with carbon blued Damascus blade and bolsters. Opener button in solid gold with amber, mammoth fossil ivory slabs with amber eyes, scrimshaw by Mirella Pachi.
Overall length 7" (178 mm).
"Folding Utility", 2004
Liner lock with carbon blued Damascus blade and bolsters. Opener button in solid gold with white diamond, mammoth fossil ivory slabs. Scrimshaw of Jan Cohen's horse "Magic Moment" by Mirella Pachi.
Overall length 7" (178 mm).

Opposite page, from the top:
Dietmar Kressler, Germany, *2005*
Tail lock interframe folder with antique tortoise shell. RWL34 stainless steel blade and handle. Mechanism fabricated by Christian Rankl. Scrimshaw on tortoise shell (very rare) by Lori Ristinen.
Overall length 7" (178 mm).
Jess Horn, South Africa, *1993*
Stainless steel lockback folder with ivory scales. Scrimshaw by "Garbo" (Gary Williams).
Overall length 8" (203 mm).
Kaj Embretsen, Sweden, *1994*
Mammoth ivory interframe lockback folder made of Damasteel forged by maker. Scrimshaw by Rick Fields.
Overall length 6 1/2" (165 mm).

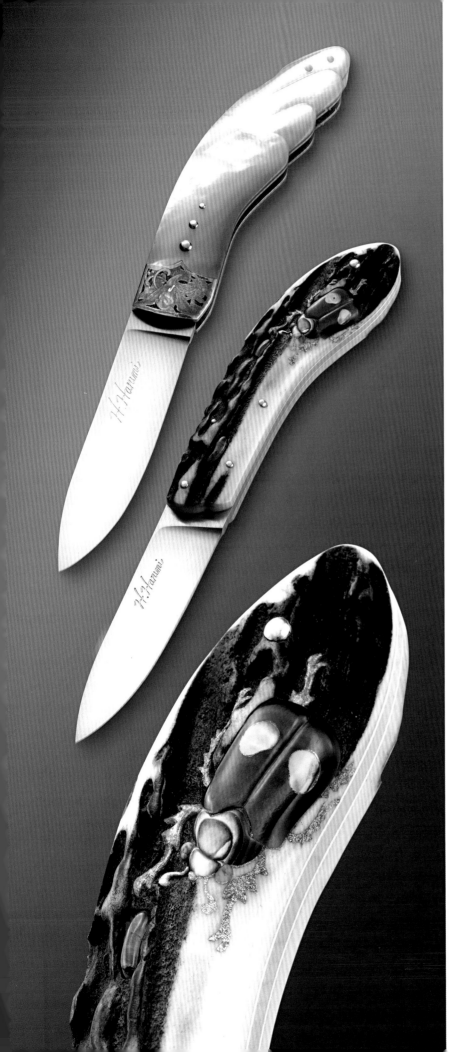

Left, from the top:
Harumi Hirayama, Japan
"Swan Series" #1, 1984
The first knife designed by Harumi.
Lockback Mother-of-Pearl folder
with 18k gold pins. Silver bolsters
and silver liners. Hummingbird
engraved by John Robyn.
Overall length 5 1/4" (133 mm).
"Pico Series, Beetle Knife", 2005
Fixed blade. 440C blade, silver liners,
stag handle and 18k gold pins.
Beetle constructed with Black-lip
pearl, abalone, malachite and 24k
gold thread.
Overall length 5 1/4" (133 mm).

Opposite page, from the left:
Tim Herman, USA
"Lockback Interframe", 2003
Black-lip pearl interframe folder,
with marine aquatic scene color
engraved by maker. Created for the
2003 AKI Show.
Overall length 6 1/4" (159 mm).
Joe Kious, USA
"Model 6", 2004
416 stainless steel lockback, Black-
lip pearl interframe folder, ATS 34
stainless steel blade. Color engraved
parrots by Ray Cover Jr., his first
color engraved knife.
Overall length 6 1/4" (159 mm).

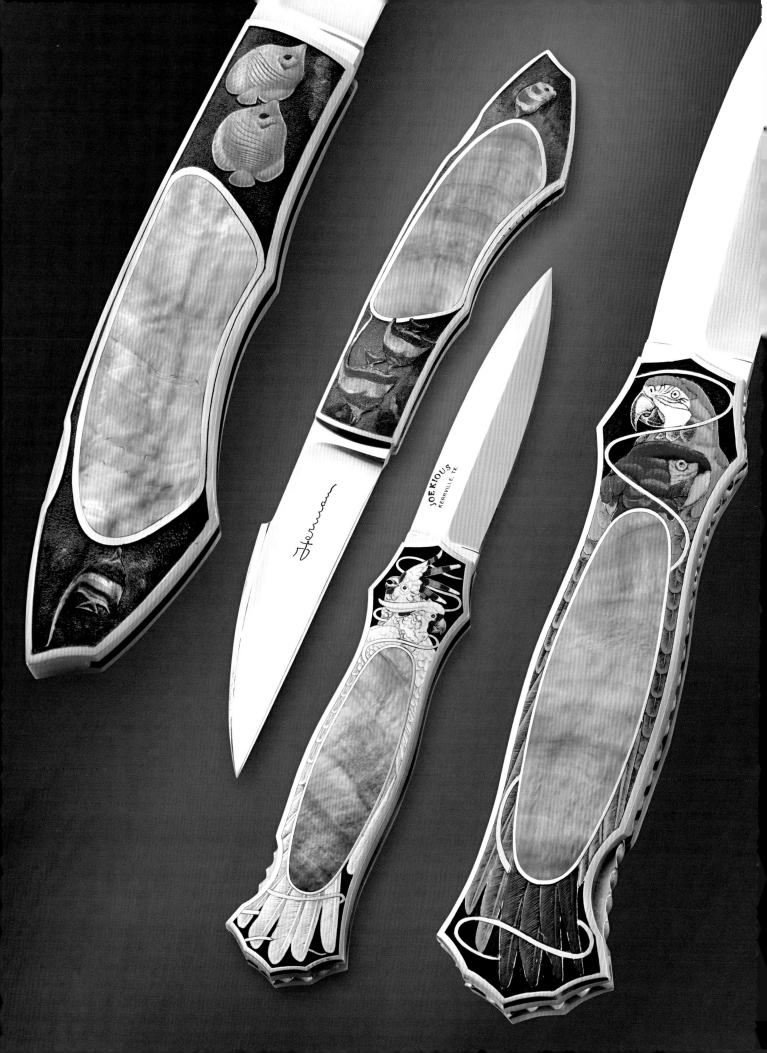

Left, from the top:
Dietmar Kressler, Germany
"Art knife", 2005
Fixed-blade knife with a fully carved
fossilized walrus ivory handle,
Damasteel blade and silver bolster.
Overall length 10" (254 mm).
Stephen Olszewski, USA
"Jan's Horse", 2004
Liner lock folder created in the image
of Jan Cohen's horse. Mammoth
ivory scales, Jerry Rados Rosebud
Damascus bolsters, blued Rados
Ladder pattern Damascus blade,
fileworked and blued titanium liners.
Thumbstud with blue sapphire.
Screws, halter, bail and eyes (with
cognac diamonds) all in 14k gold.
Overall length 8 1/2" (216 mm).

Opposite page, from the left:
Knives by Joe Kious, USA
"Model 6A Pocket Locket", 2004
Lockback antique tortoise interframe.
Mike Norris Ladder pattern Damascus
blade. Locket plate in stainless steel.
24k gold relief engraving by Ron
Skaggs.
Overall length 6 1/4" (159 mm).
"Model 6 Double Pocket Locket", 2005
Lockback stainless steel folder. Mike
Norris Ladder pattern Damascus
blade. Locket plates in 18k rose gold.
Engraved by Ray Cover Jr.
Overall length 6 1/4" (159 mm).

Joe Kious and Dr. David Cohen

Above, from the left:
Harumi Hirayama, Japan
"Pico Series", 2005
Featured are two knives from Harumi's lovely "Pico" series. The first is a ***"Dragonfly Lockback"*** folder with an ironwood handle and dragonfly Inlays. The bolsters are silver. Overall length 6 1/4" (159 mm). The second knife of this series is ***"The Butterfly Lockback"*** folder with a mastodon ivory handle with butterfly Inlays. The bolsters are silver. Both knives have assorted inlays of shell, stone, wood, coral, gold and silver. Overall length 5 1/4" (133 mm).

Opposite page, from the top:
Juergen Steinau, Germany
Model "LBS" (lockback small), 2005
X40Cr13 stainless steel blade with 18k gold insert with pearl, stone and bakelite inlays.
Overall length 6 1/4" (159 mm).
Model "Straight", 1992
440B-X90CrMoV18 blade, pure nickel inserts, Mother-of-Pearl and buffalo horn inlays.
Overall length 7 1/4" (184 mm).
Model "LBM" (lockback medium), 2004
RWL 34 blade, nicorros inserts, Mother-of-Pearl, bakelite and stone inlays.
Overall length 9" (228 mm).
Model "LBL" (lockback long), 2005
RWL 34 blade, nicorros inserts. MOP, bakelite and stone inlays.
Overall length 14 3/4" (375 mm).
Model "SB" (switchblade), 1994
440B-X90CrMoV18 blade, stainless steel handle, mammoth ivory inserts inlaid with 18k gold figures.
Overall length: 8 1/2" (216 mm).
Model "SB" (switchblade), 1991
Designed to be used in the desert. 440B-X90CrMoV18 blade, stainless steel handle. Pure nickel inserts with buffalo horn, pearl, opal and hematite inlays.
Overall length 8 1/2" (216 mm).
Model "CU" (Cutter), 2000
440B-X90CrMoV18 blade, stainless steel handle, MOP and Black-lip pearl inlays.
Overall length 7 1/2" (190 mm).

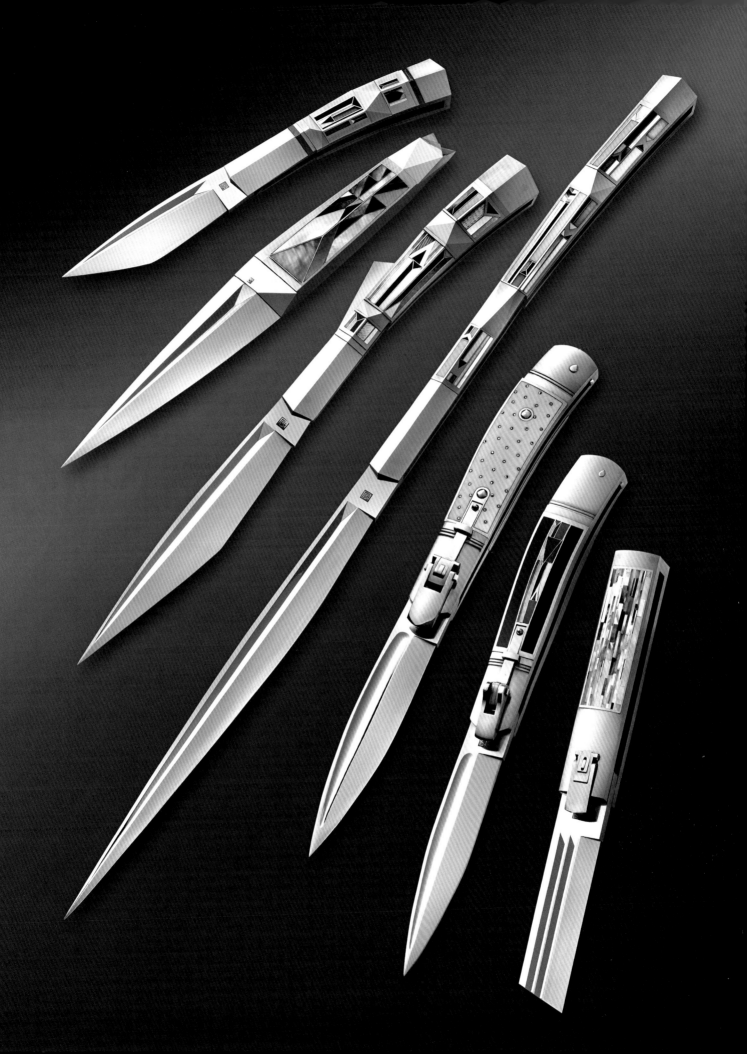

Opposite page, from the left:

Wolfgang Loerchner, Canada
"Stainless Steel Lock Back", late '90s
Mother-of-Pearl inlay. Fully sculpted frame and pearl.
Overall length 6 1/4" (159 mm).

"Persian Lock Back Folder", 2000
Stainless steel frame with Damascus and Black-lip pearl inlay's. Fully sculpted handle and blade.
"Wolf's interpretation of a Folding Persian is unrivaled"!
Overall length 7 3/4" (197 mm).

"Folding Dagger", 2001
Stainless steel frame with Damascus and Black-lip pearl Inlays. Rear lock. Fully sculpted frame with partly carved Damascus blade.
"A Folder Fit For a King"!
Overall length 7 1/4" (184 mm).

"Folding Dagger", 2001
Stainless steel frame with Damascus inlay and pearl escutcheon. Pearl overlay on lock release button. Stainless blade with Damascus inlay. Fileworked rear bolster.
Overall length 7 1/4" (184 mm).

"Sculpted Lock Back", 2001
Stainless steel frame and blade. Carved wings and blade.
"Symmetry comes together to make this one of my favorite Loerchner folders".
Overall length 7" (178 mm).

Dave Ellis *USA*

I have a passion for knives! I collect, buy and sell knives. As a Mastersmith with the American Bladesmith Society, I have also chosen to create knives. I truly live and breathe knives on a daily basis. My interest goes back to my childhood, when I carried a fine Barlow, then it was Puma, in particular the Folding Hunter style. In the mid Eighties, I discovered the world of custom knives and I was hooked. I collected anything and everything. I also found that someday I may need to sell some of my prized "toys". As luck (and much research) would have it, I now know that my primary choices were sound. I was buying Bob Loveless and Bill Moran knives mostly. Some years I could only afford one or two, other years I would sell some, buy some and after a short time put together a nice collection of both maker's works. I currently focus on Bob Loveless, Bill Moran, Ron Lake, Michael Walker and Jim Schmidt for the investment portfolio and personally collect Wolfgang Loerchner folders for their value, both intrinsic and monetary. Wolf's flowing lines and artistic handwork make him one of my favorite makers. Through my Websites, *http://www.exquisiteknives.com* and *http://www.mastersmith.com*, I hope to further this craft and be able to offer the public some rare or never-before-seen pieces of modern knifemaking at it's finest.

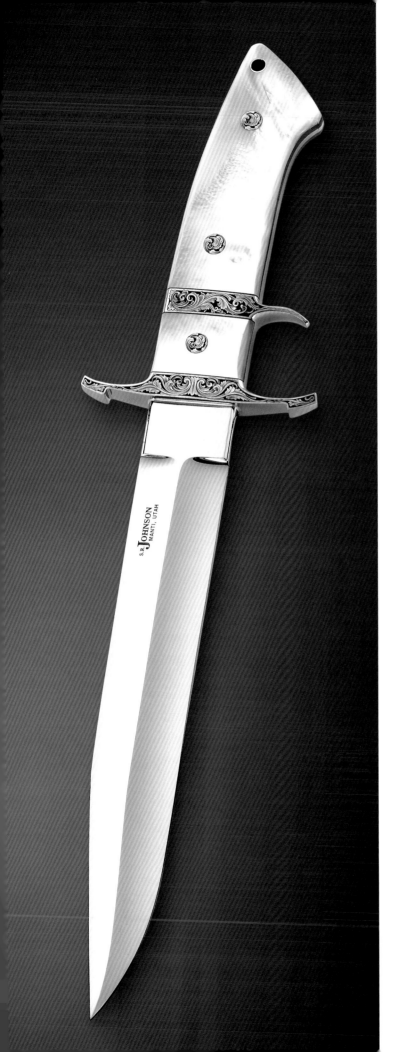

Left:

Steve. R. Johnson, USA
"Pearl Big Bear", 2001
Enormous Mother-of-Pearl slabs,
supplied by the collector were used
for the handle of this magnificent
knife. After winning "best of show"
award at the 2001 Solvang Show, the
knife was shipped of to be engraved
and gold inlaid by Steve Lindsay.
Overall length 14" (356 mm).

Opposite page:

**Steve. R. Johnson (USA) and Firmo
Fracassi (Italy)**
"The African Big Five", mid '80s
This is a series of five Classic Hunters
made by S.R. Johnson with stainless
steel blades, bolsters and pins. Bark
ivory scales show all of the battle
scars and weathered surfaces, truly
accentuating this one of a kind set.
Bolsters engraved by Firmo Fracassi
(Italy). One side with a full study of
the animal, the other with a close-up
study. Even the pins are engraved
with details of the settings. Blades
on all knives are 3 1/2" (89 mm), and
Overall length is 8" (203 mm).
*"I have only been able to acquire
three of these masterpieces, the
elephant is #1 of 5, the lion #2 of 5
and the water buffalo is #5 of 5.
I hope to acquire the other two
pieces, the leopard and the
rhinoceros."*

Left, from the top:

Michael Walker, USA

"Crescent Blade-lock", late '90s

Anodized pivot. Stainless blade and frame. Michael Walker's patented blade lock is as smooth as silk. Push to unlock and open, push to unlock and close.

Overall length 6" (152 mm).

"D-lock", mid '90s

This is an ivory interframe with stainless steel blade and anodized screws. Roller on bottom facilitates one handed blade opening.

Overall length 6 3/16" (162 mm).

"D-Lock", mid '90s

All titanium frame and stainless steel blade. Patricia Walker's engraving shows Earth on one side, and Atlas holding Earth on the other.

Overall length 6 3/16" (162 mm).

Opposite page, from the top:

Michael Walker, USA

"Large Blade Lock", 2001

Damascus blade. Two piece, dovetail connected handle of Stamascus and titanium. Turbine style bolster.

Overall length 9" (229 mm).

"D-Lock", 2005

This knife was made for the 2005 Art Knife Invitational Show in San Diego. Damascus blade, Turbine style bolster. Gold and assorted inlays in the handle.

Overall length 7 1/4" (184 mm).

"Blade Lock", late '90s

Damascus blade and frame. Gold and assorted inlays in the handle.

Overall length 6 1/4" (159 mm).

Above:

Bob Loveless, USA

"Stag Dagger Set", 2005

Three daggers, all with stainless steel hilts and sambar stag handles. The blades are approximately 4 1/2" (114 mm), 5 1/2" (140 mm) and 6 1/2" (165 mm) in length.

"Symmetrical dagger s from the Loveless shop are very rare as most of his double edged models are asymmetrical. I chose the Loveless/ Merritt logo as I am friendly with Jim Merritt who works along Bob in the Loveless shop. Two of my personal heros."

Opposite page, from the top:

James Schmidt, USA

"Slow Ride", 1998

A triple bolstered (blackened Damascus used in the bolsters), small sized folding knife. Tortoise scales inset with gold pins. Tail lock with gold bail. The spine is fully fileworked as are the liners. Damascus blade.

Overall length 6 1/2" (165 mm).

"Kidney Pie", 1995

Starburst, blackened Damascus bolsters are a key feature of this large tail lock folding fighter. The Mother-of-Pearl scales have gold pins and the rear of the pearl protrudes as "Persian Ears" beyond the knife frame. Gold bail and a Damascus blade. Spine and liners beautifully fileworked.

Overall length 9" (229 mm).

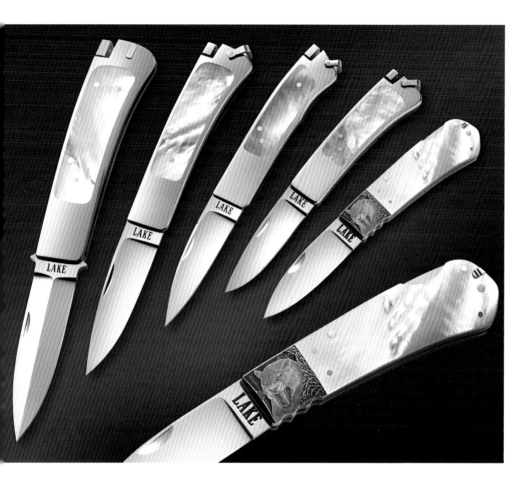

Above, from the left:

Ron Lake, USA

"Folding Fighter", late '90s

Stainless steel interframe with Mother-of-Pearl, tail lock design. Integral guard. Rose gold screws and eyeglass screwdriver (a very rare feature). Double ground blade. Overall length 7 1/2" (190 mm). The knife has a rare reverse logo on its backside, indicating that it is from the Art Knife Invitational.

"Interframe Folder", late '90s

Mother-of-Pearl inlay with gold screws and stainless steel bail. Tail-lock design. Overall length 6" (152 mm).

"Orion", mid '90s

Black-lip pearl interframe. Gold screws and bail. Tail lock design. 5 1/4" (133 mm). *"Simply perfection in a folding knife"!*

"Interframe Folder in 18k", late '80s

Solid gold frame and screws, with amazing Mother-of-Pearl inlays. Gold bail. Tail lock design. Overall length 4 1/2" (114 mm). *"This Knife was featured on the cover of Blade Magazine".*

Lock Back Folder, mid '90s

Mother-of-Pearl scales. Sculpted bolsters with engraving of large cats by Pedretti (Italy). Toothpick inset in the rear of pearl scale. Overall length 5 1/2" (140 mm).

Opposite page, from the left:

Bill Moran, USA

"Large Newer Design Bowie", late '90s

A very large Bowie, forged from round-bar steel with an Integral bolster. Fileworked guard with two pierced heart shapes. Coffin shaped curly maple handle, inset with silver wire and a nickel-silver small butt cap. The blade is 14" (356 mm), and Overall length 19" (482 mm).

"Fighter", 1991

50 years, stamped St-24 (a special stamp Bill Moran used on only 50 knives, to celebrate his 50th year of knifemaking). Bill's smaller version of the St-24. Forged 5160 blade, fileworked nickel-silver hilt, curly maple handle inset with silver wire and carved oak leaves on top of handle. Overall length 12 1/2" (317 mm). *"This knife was used in one of the Bill Moran Videos".*

"Gentleman's Fighter", late '90s

Blade is forged out of round-bar steel with a fileworked Integral bolster. Fileworked nickel-silver guard and a different handle shape made of curly maple with silver wire inlay and a rare ivory ferrule. Overall length 13" (330 mm). *"Bill's Gent's Fighter is truly light and quick in the hand".*

"Damascus Fighter", 1994

50 years, stamped St-24 Ladder pattern Damascus Blade. Fileworked with two pierced hearts in the nickel-silver guard. Curly maple grip with silver wire inlay. Overall length 15 1/2" (394 mm). *"This is an all-out Bill Moran Damascus fighting knife, very light for its size and it also has one of the sharpest edges ever"!*

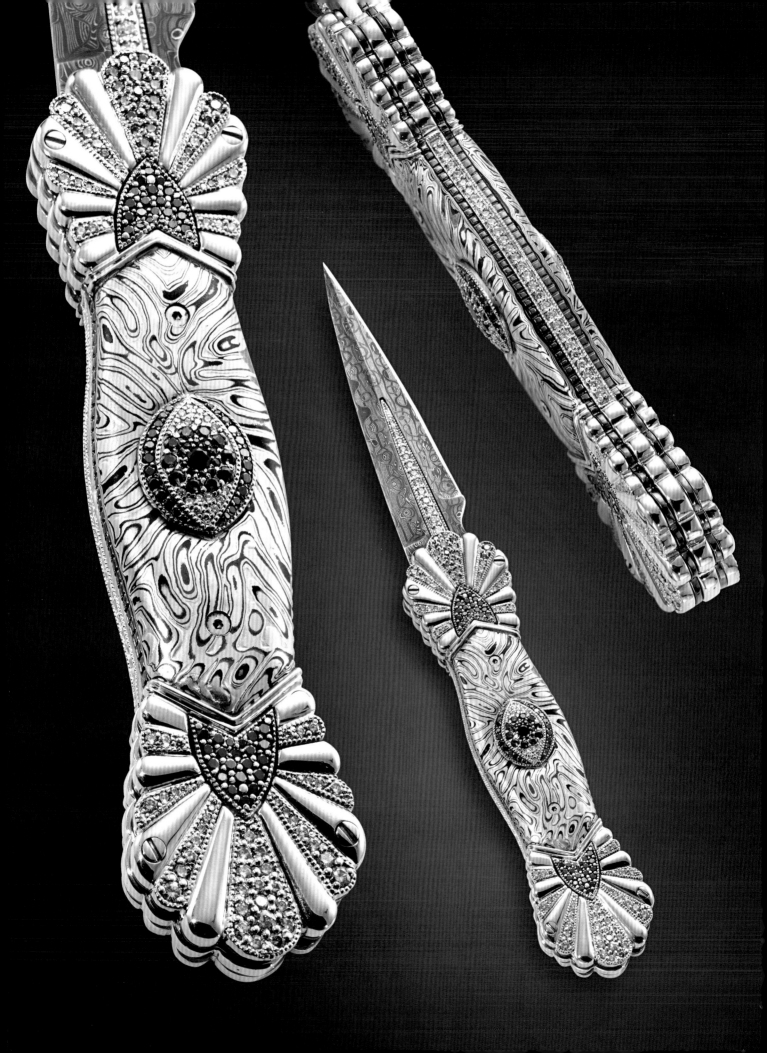

Jeff Gale USA

Opposite page:
Kenneth King, USA
"Eye of God" Auto, 2006
Handle is made of 18k yellow and pink gold mokume with contrasting shakudo layers and 420 set diamonds, sapphires and black diamonds. The blade is Sunstorm Damascus by Mike Norris and is inlaid with 18k gold strips that are set with 30 diamonds (round pave set), measuring from 3.5 to 2 mm. The "Eye" in the handle is made of 18k white gold designed in a "pave and channel" setting style. Center is a 4 point round sapphire surrounded by 20 2.5/1.5 mm sapphires pave set. Sides of the eye are 40 1.5 mm white diamonds; its outer edges have 24 round black diamonds. Bolster and pommels are made of 18k yellow and white gold and set with 156 round pave set diamonds from 3.5 to 1.5 mm in size as well as 76 2.25 mm round black diamonds. The spine is made of 18k gold set with 28 2.25 mm round white diamonds. Overall length 11 3/4" (298 mm).

In 1995, while touring the Uffizi Museum in Florence, Italy, and gazing at such works of art as Botticelli's Venus, Jeff Gale thought he had seen the finest masterpieces in the world. It wasn't until he wandered into G. Lorenzi in Milan that he realized that for him, true art was to be found in the intricate engraving and functionality of the knives carried in this little corner store on the famed Via Napoleone. Until that day, Jeff had no idea such beauty could be found on such dangerous weapons. Returning to the United States, Jeff attended The Knife Guild Show in Las Vegas. There he met the flamboyant knife collector, Ed Wormser of Chicago. The two men hit it off immediately and Ed became not only a good friend, but an important mentor as well, teaching him the who's who of the knife-making world. As with all passions, a fire was lit and Jeff Gale has fanned the flames of his desire, seeking out the most famous knife makers and challenging them to design in precious materials such as gold and diamonds. One of the first knives Kenneth King made for him was a design collaboration between the two men and contains a pound of gold and 450 set white diamonds, black diamonds and sapphires.

This page, from the left:

Jimmy Lile, USA

"Jimmy Lile (1934-1991), "The Arkansas Knifemaker" is known worldwide for the quality of his work. The knives are still made by the craftsmen he trained, with his widow inspecting each piece before it is sold. Lile was the creator of the original "Rambo First Blood" and "Rambo II the Mission" knives that were actually used in the first two "Rambo" movies. Lile is the inventor and craftsman of the patented "Lile Lock" folding knife, which is proudly on display at the Smithsonian Institute.

"Auto #1", 1979

3/4 lock folding hunter. Engraving by James Stewart. Brass handle with craved ivory inlays. Stainless steel blade.
Overall length 6 1/4" (158 mm).

"3/4 Lile", 2001

3/4 lock folding hunter. Engraving by Julie Warenski. Handle is nickel-silver with Gold-lip pearl inlays. Stainless steel blade.
Overall length 6 1/4" (158 mm).

Opposite page, from the top:

Jimmy Lile, USA

"Large Lock Folding Hunter", 1979

Pre-patented interframe, engraved by James Stewart. Brass handle with carved (sheep and cougar) ivory inlays. Stainless steel blade.
Overall length 8 1/4" (209 mm).

"Large Lock Folding Hunter", 1979

Pre-patented interframe, engraved by James Stewart. Stainless steel handle with carved (fly fishing and beaver) ivory inlays. Stainless steel blade.
Overall length 8 1/4" (209 mm).

"Large Lock Folding Hunter", 1979

Pre-patented interframe, engraved by James Stewart. Nickel-silver handle with carved ivory inlays and 14k gold ducks. Stainless steel blade.
Overall length 8 1/4" (209 mm).

On the left:
Jimmy Lile, USA
"Bowie", 1987
Deep relief engraving by G.R.
Blanchard. Ivory handle.
Overall length 13 3/4 (342 mm).

Opposite page, from the left:
Lloyd Hale, USA
"Large Bowie", 2004
Abalone and Black-lip pearl handle
with Kenneth King settings of 18k
gold, diamonds and sapphires. 440C
stainless steel blade.
Overall length 17 7/8" (454 mm).
"Large Sub Hilt Bowie" 2004
Gold-lip pearl and abalone handle.
440C stainless steel blade.
Overall length 17 7/8" (454 mm).

On the left:
Lloyd Hale. USA
"Hunter with Sheath", 2003
Knife and nickel-silver sheath engraved and gold inlaid by Julie Warenski. Blade is 440C stainless steel. Handle with Mother-of-Pearl and Gold-lip pearl.
Overall length 9 1/2" (241 mm).

Opposite page:
Lloyd Hale, USA
"Large Serpentine ", 2005
Handle with Gold-lip pearl, Mother-of-Pearl, abalone and fossilized coral. Blade is 440C stainless steel.
Overall length 21" (533 mm).

This page, from the top:

Joe Kious, USA

"Auto Model 4", 2002

Handle is 18k pink gold with gold bail, both completely carved and engraved by Julie Warenski with black and white diamonds and rubies. Black steel overlay is carved in 3D. Robert Eggerling Damascus blade steel with rope pattern file-worked spine.

Overall length 7 3/4" (197 mm).

"Tomb Raider" Auto, 2004

Engraving by Ron Skaggs, Robert Eggerling Damascus blade, stainless steel handle with 24k gold, sterling silver and copper.

Overall length 9" (228 mm).

Opposite page, from the left:

Jim Martin (USA) for Barrett Smythe

Handle is solid 18k gold with diamonds and emeralds. Stainless steel blade engraved and gold inlaid.

Overall length 6 5/8" (168 mm).

Joe Kious, USA

"Auto Model 4", 2006

18k solid gold handle with gem quality lapis inlays. Engraving by Julie Warenski with white diamonds, sapphires and black diamonds. Diamond studded solid gold toothpick. Mike Norris Stainless Damascus.

Overall length 7" (178 mm).

"Auto", 2000

18k gold handle with Black-lip pearl inlays. Engraving and platinum inlay by Tim George. Mike Norris, stainless Damascus blade.

Overall length 7" (178 mm).

Dellana, USA

"Magic Maker", 1999

The blade is composite Damascus steel forged by Dellana. Handle is 14k pink gold with diamonds. Bolsters and lock bar "saddle" are fabricated of 14k yellow gold that is first fused, then formed and forged by hand (by Dellana) to create a unique "melted" look.

Overall length 6 3/8" (162 mm).

This page, from the top:

Kenneth King, USA

"Warncliffe Auto", 2005

Mokume handle made of 18k yellow gold layered with shakudo, with an 18k gold button inlaid with Australian opal in its center. Bolster and pommel are inset with 14k gold textured strips flush-set with 2.5 mm sapphires and diamonds. Kenneth King "pool & eye" Ladder pattern Damascus blade, made of 1095. 0-1 and nickel. 18k yellow gold thumb stud inset with a center sapphire and surrounded with pave diamonds. Overall length 8 1/2" (216 mm).

George Dailey, USA

"Auto", 2000

Engraving by Julie Warenski, Gold-lip pearl handle 18k gold inlays and white diamonds. Daryl Meier Damascus blade steel.
Overall length 7 1/2" (190 mm).

"Auto", 1999

Engraving by Ray Cover Jr., Mother-of-Pearl handle with sapphire, diamonds and gold inlays. Blade Damascus by George Worth.
Overall length 7 1/2" (190 mm).

Opposite page, from the left:

Kenneth King, USA

"Purple Heart", 2003/2004

Sterling silver handle of a "Thru-bolt" type construction, with 2 carved Mother-of-Pearl insets each with a single 5ct round amethyst bezel set in 18k gold. Kenneth King carved Ladder pattern Damascus blade made of 1095 and nickel with an inlaid textured strip of 18k gold. The blade is also set with an 18k heart of 50 round diamonds surrounding 34 3-3.5 mm amethysts, set in a Cartier style prong mounting.
Overall length 21 1/2" (546 mm).

"Persian Fighter", 2004

Oxidized sterling silver handle with carved Gold-lip pearl. Pearl is center set with a square emerald surrounded by 16 pave set .025 diamonds in white gold. Bolster and pommel are hand fabricated of 14k gold and tricolor mokume of 18k yellow, white and pink gold with contrasting black layers of shakudo. Both have a carved and fluted guard plate made of hot-blued 1018 steel. Pommel has an 18ct oval black star sapphire mounted in an 18k gold scalloped bezel.
Overall length 15 1/2" (394 mm).

Opposite page, from the left:
Joe Kious, USA
"Window Knife", 1997
Engraved for Barrett Smythe by
Lee R. Griffiths. 440C stainless steel
handle inset with green topaz over
engraved with wild boar scenes by
Creative Art of Italy.
Overall length 5 3/4" (146 mm).
E. G. Peterson, USA
"Mini Executive", 1996
Stainless steel handle and blade
engraved by Chris Meyer with Black-
lip pearl inlays and 18k gold nuggets.
Overall length 5 5/8" (143 mm).

On the right:
Steve Olszewski, USA
"Golden Rose", 2005
18k solid gold handle over tortoise
shell. Jerry Rados Turkish Damascus
blade steel.
Overall length 6 1/2" (165 mm).

Opposite page, from the left:
Lloyd Hale, USA
"Sub-Hilt Fighter", 2004
Black ebony inlaid with Mother-of-
Pearl, encased by nickel-silver. Blade and
fittings are 440C stainless steel.
Overall length 13 1/2" (343 mm).
Bob Loveless, USA
"Big Bear", mid '90s
Black micarta handle and stainless steel.
Overall length 14" (356 mm).
"Fighter", late '90s
Stag handle and stainless steel.
Overall length 9 1/4" (235 mm).
"Utility Hunter", late '90s
Wood handle with engraved brass bolster,
pins and inlays. Stainless steel blade.
Overall length 8 1/2" (216 mm).

On the right:
Bob Loveless, USA
"Wilderness", mid '90s
Micarta handle, bolster and pins
engraved by Dan Wilkerson, stainless
steel blade.
Overall length 10 3/4" (273 mm).

This page, from the left:

Joe Kious, USA

"Auto Pocket Locket", 2002

Antique tortoises shell inlays. Handle engraved by Adone Pozzobon. Blade steel is Ladder pattern stainless Damascus by Mike Norris.
Overall length 6 1/2" (165 mm).

"Michael Price Auto Dagger", 1999

White Mother-of-Pearl handle set with 18 rubies in 18k gold bezels and two 14k gold shields. Engraving by Tim George. Mike Norris Raindrop pattern Damascus blade steel. Overall length 8 1/4" (209 mm).

Ken Steigerwalt, USA

"Auto", 2005

Carved Mother-of-Pearl handle with gold studs and and pins, 18k gold bolsters. Damascus blade. Overall length 9 3/4" (248 mm).

Joe Kious, USA

"Versace Tie Dagger", 2002

Black all steel hot blued Model 6 auto dagger engraved with 14k and 18k gold. Jerry Rados Turkish Damascus blade steel. Overall length 6 3/8" (162 mm).

Opposite page, from the top:

"Lang", Germany

"100 Blade Exhibition Knife", 2004

Stag handle 4" (102 mm) long. 100 different blades. Fully open 9 1/2" (241 mm).

"Wenger", Switzerland

"Swiss Army Exhibition Knife", 2006

Over 60 blades. Plastic handle is 3 1/4" (82 mm) long, depth (distance between handles) 8 3/4" (222 mm). Fully open it is 8 1/2" (216 mm).

Opposite page, from the top:

Stephen Olszewski, USA

"Stephen was a top designer for Este Lauder compacts, museum replicas, Franklin Mint and others. About 10 years ago he discovered art knives and soon became a full time maker".

"Horse Folder", 2004

Rados Ladder pattern Damascus blade, Rados Turkish Damascus bolsters, mammoth ivory scales. 14k gold eyes, gold screws and thumb stud.
Overall length 8 1/2" (216 mm).

"Eagle Auto", 2004

George Werth Damascus blade, Daryl Meier Random pattern Damascus bolsters. Carved walrus scales, gold screws and selective hot blueing for accents.
Overall length 9" (228 mm).

"Cockatoo Auto", 2002

Eggerling Damascus blade, Daryl Meier Random pattern Damascus bolsters. Green mammoth ivory scales. Gold screws and gold eyes with emeralds.
Overall length 8 1/2" (216 mm).

"Golden Eagle", 2004

Blade forged to shape Rados Turkish Damascus, bolsters are solid 14k gold, Black-lip pearl scales. Spine is 10k gold carved with feather motifs. Gold thumb stud with emerald.
Overall length 7 1/2" (190 mm).

"Grapes of Wrath", 2004

Rados Ladder pattern Damascus blade, Rados Turkish Damascus bolsters. Carved walrus scales with 14k gold inlays. Pierced blade with deep relief carving. Hidden latch, gold screws.
Overall length 11 1/2" (292 mm).

"Oak Leaf Auto Dagger", 2006

Rados Turkish Damascus blade forged to shape, deeply carved Rados Turkish Damascus bolsters. Black-lip pearl scales, gold bail. Selective etching on carved bolsters to accent leaves and acorns.
Overall length 6 1/2" (165 mm).

"Lila Deco", 2005

Scales are sterling silver with 18k yellow gold figure, 14k rose gold sash and additional inlays in 14k yellow gold. Blade is carved 440C stainless steel.
Overall length 7 1/2" (190 mm).

Don Guild *Hawaii*

Don Guild s fascination with knives began in his boyhood, 70 years ago, when one day, while playing the game of "Mumblety-peg," he lost his precious pocket knife. Later, he spent years in the antique trade favoring embellishment in all forms of applied art. Today, his eclectic knife collection runs from themes of ancient Greek mythology to modern Art-Deco. Throughout his collection one finds artfully enhanced precision-folders and fixed-blades with bas-relief carving prevalent. One of Don s passions is to research a special art theme, then engage a top knife maker and a top engraver to collaborate on it. These collaborations have resulted in several exciting art knives. For the last two years, these combined efforts have earned awards for "Best Collaboration" at the annual Atlanta Blade Show. His favorite makers and engravers hail from several foreign countries as well as from the United States. To him, the art knife world appears to have no bounds. Falling in love with art knives, and buying too many, seems to be Don s major flaw. However he keeps the excesses of this passion slightly under control through his web site. At times, in order to acquire one or two "delicious" knives, he will buy an entire knife collection or a full estate of knives. Don authored many articles about art knives that were published in *Blade Magazine*.

Opposite page, from the top:

Ken Steigerwalt, USA

"Ken's work over the years has compounded in creativity and mechanical superiority. He can deep relief carve geometrical shell shapes and angular pieces like no one else. Ken's embellishments are becoming more angular and the use of gold in his knives has elevated his work to a new level. Watch this man for even greater things to come".

"Radiant Pen Shell", 2003

This knife has pen shell for the handle, a Devin Thomas stainless Damascus blade and Eggerling Ladder pattern Damascus frame. 18k gold pins and fittings. Overall length 8" (mm).

"Wave", 2006

Black-lip pearl in the handle's 416 stainless frame, Damasteel for the blade. Inlays, button and pins are 18k yellow gold. Overall length 8" (203 mm).

"Deco Scarab", 2006

After a 1926 Cartier broach. Damasteel blade. Ron Skaggs engraved, carved and inlayed the 416 scales with 18k gold. Overall length 7 1/4" (184 mm).

Arabesque", 2006

Black-lip pearl in the 416 stainless steel frame, twisted Damasteel blade, 18k gold button and inlayed back spring. Ron Skaggs engraved, carved and inlayed the sides of the handles with gold. Overall length 9 1/4" (235 mm).

"Folies Bergere Deco", 2006

Lila Nikolska was the rage dancer of Paris in 1925. She is depicted here in 18k gold, silver and copper inlays by Ron Skaggs. ATS-34 blade and 416 stainless steel frame. Overall length 7 1/2" (190 mm).

This page, from the top:

Ken Steigerwalt (USA) and Ron Skaggs (USA)

"Make Way For Duckling", 2006

The inspiration for this knife came from the endearing "Make Way for Ducklings" book, ca 1940. Ron Skaggs engraved the feathered scales and inlayed eight gold ducklings on each side. Handle is Rados Ladder pattern Damascus and the blade is "30 Turn Twist" Damascus. Overall length 8" (203 mm).

Ray Cover Jr., USA

"Coy", 2002

"Ray Cover is well known for many years as one of the top art knife engravers. Few know how talented a knife maker he is. This is a sole authorship folder with 3D artistic rendering of lily pads and water with coy fish swimming beneath the surface".

Blade is 440C stainless steel the handle is CP titanium. Yellow colors are 24k gold, reddish colors are copper, the raised lily pads are 14k green gold. Gold on the blade is an architectural gold leaf. Overall length 6" (184 mm).

On the left:

Larry Fuegen, USA

**"Charles The Bold Unicorn Dagger",
2003**

*"Larry is one of only two knife
makers with his work on display at
the Smithsonian. Larry's commission
here was to craft a knife using the
ivory of a Narwhal tusk, which in
this case represents the horn of the
fabled unicorn. His research revealed
a unicorn horn sword in the Vienna
museum that was the most costly
sword ever made. This huge Narwhal
sword was commissioned by the
Monarch Charles the Bold in 1451.
Charles paid one million dollars for
the "unicorn horn" that was used.
Fuegen's dagger is based on this
sword and the engraved designs are
associated with the Order of the
Golden Fleece, an order of Knights
which Charles was sovereign over.
These designs represent a striker,
flint, and a shower of sparks".*
The blade is hand forged 1095
carbon steel. Handle and scabbard
are Narwhal tusk "unicorn horn".
Fittings are heavy 24k gold plating
on all engraved handle, guard, and
scabbard parts. One polished river
ruby pebble from Kenya, 6 cultured
pearls, and 2 amber cabochons.
Overall length 16" (mm).

Opposite page, from the left:

Arpad Bojtos, Slovakia

*"Arpad Bojtos is a true Renaissance
man. His "work shop" consists of
a four foot work bench, hammer,
chisel, files and sandpaper. He
even hollow grinds with hammer
and chisel. He is the only maker in
the world using only the tools of
hundreds of years ago. His historical
renderings of the Greek myths are
worthy of any museum. His sheaths
are also fully carved and complete
the story told in his knives. He makes
true classics".*

"Chameleon", 2004

Deeply hand carved ATS-34 steel
blade and moose antler handle.
Moose antler sheath with silver and
ostrich skin.
Overall length 8 1/2" (216 mm).

"Diana and Acteon", 2005

Deeply hand carved Lasky carbon
Damascus, bronze guard and stag
antler handle. Stag antler sheath
with gold, silver and ostrich skin.
Overall length 10 1/2" (267 mm).

"Cupid and Psyche", 2006

Deeply hand carved 440C blade,
inlayed with gold, copper and
titanium butterflies. Fossil walrus
ivory handle and fossil ivory
sheath with silver, gold and brown
mammoth ivory.
Overall length 10 1/4" (260 mm).

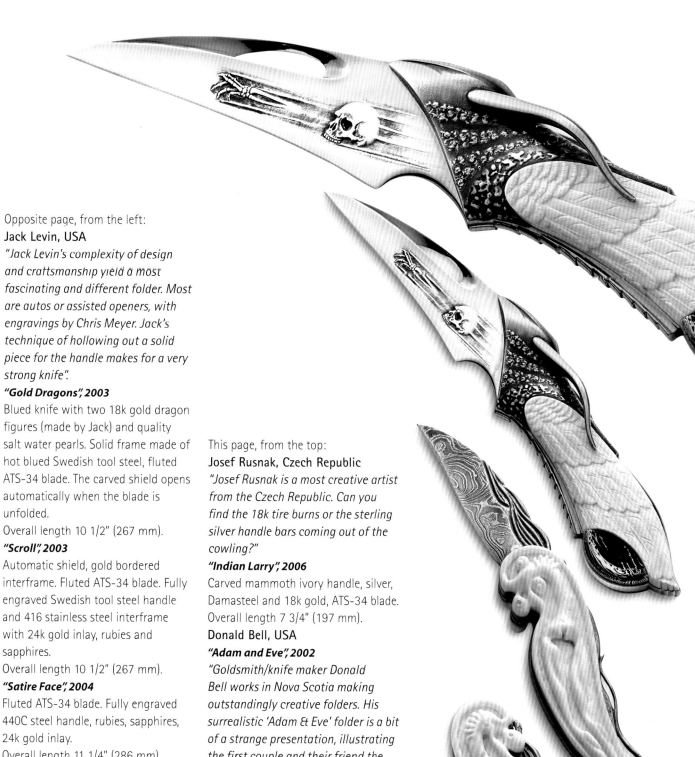

Opposite page, from the left:

Jack Levin, USA

"Jack Levin's complexity of design and craftsmanship yield a most fascinating and different folder. Most are autos or assisted openers, with engravings by Chris Meyer. Jack's technique of hollowing out a solid piece for the handle makes for a very strong knife".

"Gold Dragons", 2003

Blued knife with two 18k gold dragon figures (made by Jack) and quality salt water pearls. Solid frame made of hot blued Swedish tool steel, fluted ATS-34 blade. The carved shield opens automatically when the blade is unfolded.
Overall length 10 1/2" (267 mm).

"Scroll", 2003

Automatic shield, gold bordered interframe. Fluted ATS-34 blade. Fully engraved Swedish tool steel handle and 416 stainless steel interframe with 24k gold inlay, rubies and sapphires.
Overall length 10 1/2" (267 mm).

"Satire Face", 2004

Fluted ATS-34 blade. Fully engraved 440C steel handle, rubies, sapphires, 24k gold inlay.
Overall length 11 1/4" (286 mm).

"Small Auto", 2003

Automatic shield. Fluted Swedish stainless Damascus blade, 440C solid frame. 24k golden inlays and 303 stainless steel inlay. Various gem stones.
Overall length 8 1/4" (209 mm).

"Unicorn/Narwhal Auto", 2003

Fluted Mosaic Damascus blade with 24k gold inlay. Handle fully carve and engraved with white porcelain medallion.
Overall length 7 3/4" (197 mm).

This page, from the top:

Josef Rusnak, Czech Republic

"Josef Rusnak is a most creative artist from the Czech Republic. Can you find the 18k tire burns or the sterling silver handle bars coming out of the cowling?"

"Indian Larry", 2006

Carved mammoth ivory handle, silver, Damasteel and 18k gold, ATS-34 blade.
Overall length 7 3/4" (197 mm).

Donald Bell, USA

"Adam and Eve", 2002

"Goldsmith/knife maker Donald Bell works in Nova Scotia making outstandingly creative folders. His surrealistic 'Adam & Eve' folder is a bit of a strange presentation, illustrating the first couple and their friend the serpent, who is breathing fire that is carried into the blade with his tail flowing down the back spine. Once the blade is closed, the serpent's fiery breath becomes Eve's tumbling hair". The scale material? Oosik naturally. Blade steel is Tim Zowada's "Heavenly Body" Meteorite Damascus
Overall length 6" (152 mm).

This page, from the left:

Wolfgang Loerchner, Canada

"Wolfgang Loerchner's fixed blades and folders are a feast to the eye, especially when engraved by Martin Butler. Absolute flawlessness! He is now a full-time maker and the world of knives will be much better for that. An endless array of designs flow from this engineers mind. They are expressed on this page through his use of outstanding Damascus by Brian Lyttle, 440C steel and colorful Black-lip pearl".

"Martin's Pride", 1998
Martin Butler's engraving and 24k gold inlays depict stallions, birds and a woman's faces. 440C blade. Overall length 16 1/4" (412 mm).

"Dianna II", 1997
Martin Butler did the engraving and 24k gold inlays. 440C blade. Overall length 15 3/4" (400 mm).

Opposite page, from the left:

Jurgen Steinau, Germany

"Jurgen sees the art knife as a set of juxtapositioned complimentary angles. His work sets him aside in the art knife world and together with the fact that he makes only about ten knives each year, his are probably the rarest in the field".

"AKI Knife", 1997
A fixed-blade knife made for the 1997 Art Knife Invitational show. Nicorros inserts in handle with various inlays. Overall length 10" (254 mm).

"Gold Folder", 1996
Gold inserts with various inlays.
Overall length 8" (203 mm).

"Tortoise Shell Set", 2002-2004
A set of three knives made by Jurgen Steinau over a span of 4 years. One folding knife and two fixed-blades, all three with ancient tortoise shell inlays:

"LBM", 2004
Lock back folder wth an RWL 34 blade and X40Cr13 stainless steel handle with ancient tortoise shell inlays. Overall length 9" (229 mm)

"No. 03 05 06 . 2", 2003
A fixed-blade knife made of $X90CrMoV_{18}$ steel. Nicorros inserts in the handle with ancient tortoise shell inlays. Overall length 8 3/4" (222 mm).

"No. 02 04 21 . 2", 2002
Fixed-blade knife made of Steve Schwarzer Damascus with a "Silent Damascus finish". Nicorros inserts in the handle with ancient tortoise shell inlays.
Overall length 11 1/8" (283 mm).

Life Size

Tom and Gwen Guinn *USA*

opposite page from the top:
Yvon Vachon, Canada
Swiss Army Knives
"Champion", #1 of 2, 1998
18 blades and implements, with
33 options, 3 slide-outs (tweezers,
toothpick, ballpoint pen).
Closed length 1" (25.4 mm).
"Craftsman", #1 of 1, 1997
13 blades and implements, with
19 options, 2 slide-outs (tweezers,
toothpick). Closed length 1" (25.4 mm).
"Climber", #1 of 1, 1997
8 blades and implements, with 12
options, 2 slide-outs (tweezers and
toothpick).
Closed length 1" (25.4 mm).
*"All three of these knives were
to have been made in a Series of 6
each. Victorinox would be proud of
these! When displayed, each knife
includes its own box and instruction
sheet (proportional)".*

Welcome to our world of marvelous miniature knives. The collecting of these wonders began in August 1992 with our first custom handmade miniature knife. We were hooked! We discovered that we truly like the smaller miniature knives and strive to keep our collecting to folders of one inch or under (when closed) and three inches or under for fixed blades. An additional criterion is that a miniature knife must have proper proportions, be sharp, walk and talk, have good fit and finish and above all, bear the signature/mark of the maker! That they are very small is amazing. That they are truly functional knives is truly incredible. When we find one that takes our breaths away, we buy it. Our collection involves us both. We design the displays, build the cases, create our rosters and "mind the store" at the shows. It s a team effort all the way. The majority of our knives are one-of-a-kind miniature knives. many of the knives in our displays have won untold numbers of awards for their makers along the way (several Best of Show and Best Miniature knives). We win Display Awards almost everywhere we go. The driving force, for displaying our collection, is to educate everyone in this astounding art form. We want to share the thrill and wonder of these little beauties with the world, keeping the interest in miniature knives alive, so that they do not become an endangered species!

Life Size

Above from the top:

Yvon Vachon, Canada

"Micro Sportsman", #1 of 1, 2001

4 blades (sheep foot, buttonhook, cork screw, punch), abalone handles, gold bolster and shackle. Closed length 7/32" (5.5 mm).

"This miniature was reproduced from an antique Sportsman knife. This is the smallest of a 10-member family of same pattern but in graduated sizes".

"Congress", #1 of 1, 2000

4 blades (sheep foot, nail file and 2 pen blades) and antique tortoise handles. Length closed 21/32" (16.6 mm).

"Reproduced from an antique knife, the IXL George Wostenholm Congress".

Opposite page from the top left:

Yvon Vachon, Canada

"Mini Multi-Blade", #1 of 1, 1999

18 blades and implements, 2 slide-outs (tooth-pick and tweezers with spoon), antique tortoise handles. Closed length 1" (25.4 mm). Reproduced from an antique H. Cromwill Criterion knife.

"Because most of the nail nicks on the blades are tiny, Yvon made a blade opening tool as shown on the left".

"Exclusive Model", 2000 & 2001

5 different sizes, made exclusively for this collection and reproduced from an antique Henry Hobson & Son/Sheffield knife. 6 blades and implements, antique tortoise handles with 10k white gold bolsters, 10k yellow gold liners. Closed lengths: 1 1/2" (39 mm), 1" (25.4 mm), 5/8" (16 mm), 1/2" (13 mm), 3/8" (9.5 mm).

Yvon Vachon
Quebec, Canada

"Yvon Vachon's reputation for being one of the most talented miniature and micro-miniature knife makers in the world came early in his endeavors. Our odyssey into his world of miniatures began at the Blade Show in Atlanta, Georgia, USA in 1995, when we ordered our first Vachon creation. It was his first show in the U.S.

Yvon was French-Canadian from Quebec, Canada and spoke little or no English at the time. He depended on an ancient jewelers lathe for precision rather than to use a pantograph or milling machines. The bulk of his pieces were made tediously by hand, with passion and a driving concern for correctness. He was always saying, "It is correct?" The more complicated the knife, the more he was challenged (i.e., black-powder guns, multi-bladed miniatures). He was energetic and intense and could also be very comical. We always laughed a lot when we were together.

Yvon Vachon died much too young, at age 46, on October 9, 2001. The very small knife on this page is the smallest and the last one he ever made.

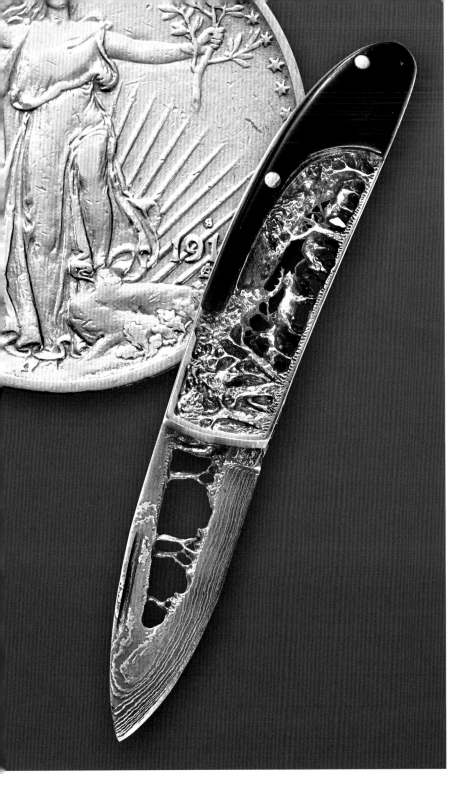

Life Size

Opposite page, counter-clockwise, from left of the coin:

Jim Whitehead, Oregon, USA
Sword, 2005
With a 2 7/8" (73 mm) Damascus blade. Guard, handle and pommel made of 18k gold and ivory, are all carved and engraved.
Overall length 3 3/4" (95 mm).

"Bat" Sword, 2002
Has a 2 3/16" (55 mm) blade. Guard, handle and pommel of 18k gold and ivory, are all carved and engraved.
Overall length 3 3/16" (81 mm).

Sword, 2002
Has a 1 7/8" (50 mm) engraved blade. Guard and pommel are 18k gold carved and engraved. Handle is ivory.
Overall length 2 3/4" (70 mm).

Silver Bowie, 1998
With a 1 15/16" (49 mm) Damascus blade. Metal surfaces are engraved on all sides, including the sheath. Guard and handle are 7 pieces silver and ivory, pommel is silver.
Overall length 3 1/16" (78 mm).

Coffin Handle Bowie, 2002
With a 2 1/16" (52 mm) blade. Metal surfaces are engraved on all sides, including the sheath. Guard and handle are of 18k gold and ivory with 18k gold pins.
Overall length 3 3/8" (86 mm).

"Heart and Soul", Bowie 1997
With 2 3/8" (60 mm) Damascus blade. Guard and handle are 13 pieces silver, 18k gold and mastodon ivory. with silver pommel, all engraved all over.
Overall length 4 1/4" (108 mm) in the engraved silver and 18k gold sheath.

Above:
Charles Roulin, Geneva, Switzerland
"Deers", 1998
Stag Scene Folder with a 3/4" (19 mm) Damascus blade in which trees are hand carved upside down in the metal. The scales are water buffalo, with deer (2 stag, 6 does) carved out of the metal portion.
Closed length 1 1/16" (27 mm).

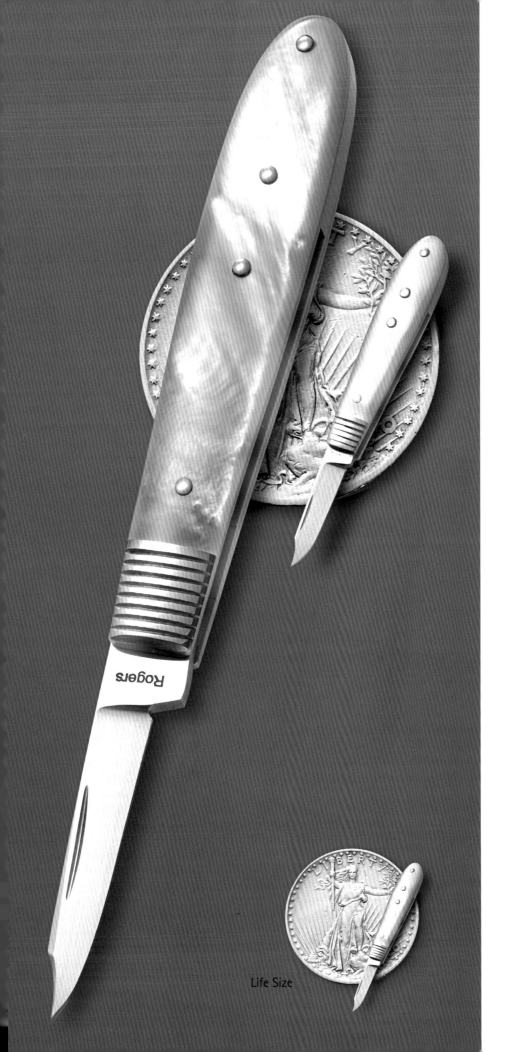

Life Size

On the left:
Richard Rogers, New Mexico, USA
"George Washington Quill Knife"
(full-size), 2003
With a 1 11/16" (49 mm) blade.
Handle is Mother-of-Pearl with
domed pins, threaded bolster.
Closed length 3" (76 mm).
Miniature "George Washington
Quill Knife", 2003
With a 9/16" (14 mm) blade, Mother-
of-Pearl handle, domed pins, threaded
bolster. Closed length 1 1/16" (27 mm).

Opposite page, from the top:
Jim Martin, California, USA
"Pirate Knife" (full size), 1993
With a 3 3/4" (95 mm) blade, pink
Mother-of-Pearl inlays. Engraved by
Gil Rudolph.
Closed length 4" (102 mm).

Miniature Folders:
Pirate Lock Back (#01), 1994
With a 3/4" (19 mm) blade, Mother-
of-Pearl handle, gold pins, gold
inlay. Pirate face on front, skull and
cross bones on back. Engraved by Gil
Rudolph. Closed length 1" (25.4 mm).
Gold Lock Back (#02), 1993
With a 3/4" (19 mm) blade. Handle
is 18k gold, Black-lip pearl inlay.
Engraved by Gil Rudolph.
Closed length 1" (25.4 mm).
Liner Lock (#01), 2002
With a 3/4" (19 mm) blade. Handle is
nickel-silver, Black-lip pearl inlay,
sapphire thumb stud. Top edge of
blade, back spring and lock spring
engraved. Engraving by maker.
Closed length 1" (25.4 mm).
Lock Back (#02), 1993
With a 3/4" (19 mm) blade. Handle
is nickel-silver with abalone inlay.
Engraved by Gil Rudolph. Closed
length 1" (25.4 mm).
"Jim Martin and Gil Rudolph were
friends. Because of Gil's art talents,
Jim encouraged him to learn
engraving; later, Gil taught Jim to
engrave. Turnabout's fair play".

On the left:

Al Eaton, California, USA
"Jonathan Crooks Bowie" #01, 1997
Handle is simulated stag, leather-over-wood sheath with silver throat and point.
Overall length 3 15/16" (100 mm) in the sheath.

Charles Weiss, Arizona, USA
"Michael Price Bowie" #01, 1997
With blued 01 steel handle, nickel silver sheath. Engraved by maker. Overall length 3 1/4" (83 mm) in the sheath.

Steven Rapp, North Carolina, USA
"Michael Price Bowie" #01, 2006
Handle is gold-in-quartz panels with 24k gold wrap, cartouche, nickel silver sheath/14k gold throat. Engraved by Julie Warenski.
Overall length 3 3/10" (84 mm) in the sheath.

Opposite page, from the top:

Glenn Waters, Japan
"Mini Butterfly" #01, 2001
Liner lock, *Shibu-ichi-gin* handle, mammoth ivory, 24k gold wire and inlay, filework.
Closed length 1" (25.4 mm).

Joseph Szilaski, New York, USA
"Carved Liner Lock", #1 of 1, 1998
Maker's Damascus handle, carved D1 steel and ivory.
Length closed 1 1/4" (32 mm).

Harumi Hirayama, Japan
*"Baby Swan "Lock Back,
#1 of 1, 2001*
Lock back folder. Mother-of-pearl handle, silver bolster, 18k gold pins.
Length closed 1 3/8" (35 mm).

Bill Ruple, Texas, USA
"Split Back Whittler" #01, 2005
Mother-of-pearl handle with nickel silver bolster, pins, 3 blades (Wharncliffe, pen, sheep foot). Two blades shown open.
Length closed 1 1/4" (32 mm).

Jim Whitehead, Oregon, USA
"Folding Liner Lock", #1 of 1, 1993
Mastodon ivory handle, Maker-engraved blade, back spring and 18k gold bolster.
Length closed 31/32" (25 mm).

H. H. Frank, Oregon, USA
*"Folding Semi-Skinner",
#1 of 1, 2000*
Engraved handle with gold inlay, 14k gold engraved bolster, hippo tooth ivory, 14k gold pins and cartouche.
Length closed 1 3/16" (30 mm).

H. H. Frank, Oregon, USA
*"Folding Italian Dagger",
#1 of 1, 2001*
Lock back, fruit knife. Handle is hippo tooth ivory. All metal parts are 14k gold and are engraved.
Length closed 1 3/16" (30 mm).

Life Size

Don Henderson USA

Born and raised on a ranch in New Mexico, I acquired an early interest in knives that has remained with me all my life. My earliest collection consisted of knives bought from hardware stores and gun shops, so one can imagine my enthusiasm when I went to my first Knife Makers Guild Show in Kansas City, in 1977. From the very first moment that I saw the knives of W. W. Cronk I was stunned by their beauty and artistry. To see the tool that has been carried by man's side for thousands of years transformed into an art form was truly a moment in my life that I will never forget. Cronk's knives were always the most expensive at the show, consequently he never sold any of his high-end pieces. Only in 1979, when my business became profitable enough, was I able to buy three of his art knives. My first of many more. *Blade Magazine* printed the facts about the sale of these high-end knives to a Florida collector, and many knifemakers later told me that this was one of the published facts that encouraged them to make high-end art knives. At a Japanese knife show I asked a well-known knifemaker, a good friend of mine, what he thought was the most difficult thing about making knives. His answer was simple: *"Coming up with new designs"*. All high-end knifemakers have to be excellent craftsmen, but coming up with new designs really sets them apart as artists. This is where W. W. Cronk excelled, and this is why he is known today as the *Father of the Art Knife*.

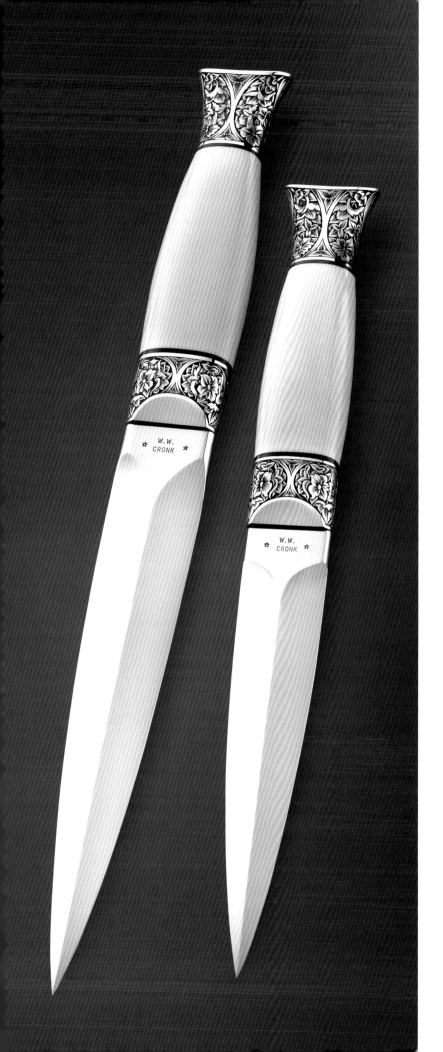

This page:
W. W. Cronk, USA,
"Ivory Pleasure", early '80s
Made of 440C stainless steel and
engraved by Ron Skaggs. Ivory handles.
_"The elegant simplicity in shape and
design of these two daggers has made
them my my favorite pair of knives"._
Overall lengths 9" (229 mm) and 11"
(279 mm).

Opposite page, from the left:
Willie Rigney, USA
"Crusader", 1991
Made after drawings and design by
W. W. Cronk. Black ebony handle.
Overall length 16" (406 mm).
"Amber Light", 1991
Made after drawings and design by
W. W. Cronk. Gold wire wrapped ivory
handle and large amethysts.
Overall length 16" (406 mm).

On the left:

W. W. Cronk, USA

"Gut Hook Fighter", early '80s

Made of 440C stainless steel and
engraved by Ron Skaggs.
Rosewood handle.
Overall length 11" (279 mm).

Opposite page, from the left:

W. W. Cronk, USA

"Fighters", early '80s

Two matching pairs made of 440C
stainless steel and engraved by Ron
Skaggs. Rosewood handles. The
Persian Pair are 11" (279 mm) long
and the *Khyber Pair* are 15"
(381 mm) long.

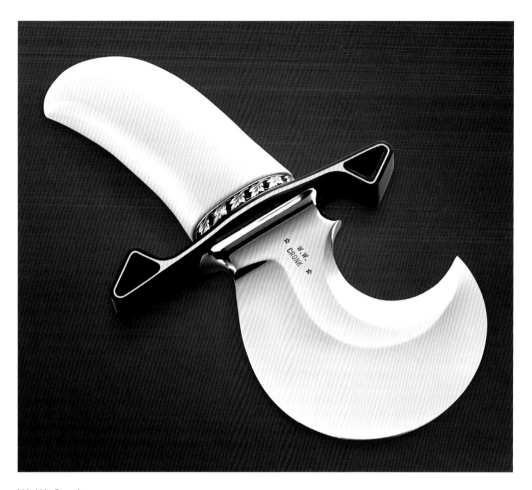

W. W. Cronk

William W. (Bud) Cronk was a machinist for the Ford Motor Co. in Greenville, Indiana. In 1963 he began making knives in his spare time. He soon tired of making simple hunting and working knives and decided to allow his imagination free rein. In 1973 Cronk was accepted as a member of the Knifemakers Guild, and soon the Guild Show was the only one he attended. At each show a crowd always gathered to gaze at his latest creations. It is hard to describe Cronk's elaborate pieces other than to call them "Art Knives". In his younger days, Cronk admitted he was influenced by comic books like "Tarzan" and "Conan", among others, where the illustrators let their imaginations run free. Although in the beginning Cronk would take special requests and work to a customer's design, he later stopped taking all orders, preferring to concentrate on "new designs and fancy one-of-a-kind pieces". All of Cronk's knives were made from 440C stainless steel with exotic woods, ivory or pearl for handles. Some were set with precious stones, and Ron Skaggs engraved most of his creations. Sadly W. W. Cronk died in early 1983, but nobody gained more recognition for this new art form than he did. It is safe to say that he is the "Father of the Art Knife". Cronk enjoyed making superbly detailed drawings of potential creations and then executing those designs into some of the most elaborate Art Knives of his generation. Willie Rigney, who was Cronk's understudy for many years and became a distinguished knifemaker in his own right, was commissioned to make some knives from Cronk's drawings as can be seen on two pages in this section. In 1984 the W. W.Cronk Memorial Art Knife Award was established in honor of his artistic and design talents. In the 23 years since that award was established it has become the most prestigious award in the world of knives. In August 2008 at the Knifemakers Guild Show in Orlando, the 25th W .W. Cronk Memorial Art Knife Award will be retired, in remembrance of a truly great artist and craftsman who has inspired generations of knifemakers to search within themselves for the passion to create a knife that can truly be called an "Art Knife".

This page:
W. W. Cronk, USA
"Alaska Delight", early '80s
Made of 440C stainless steel and engraved and gold inlaid by Ron Skaggs. Ivory handle.
Overall length 6" (152 mm).

Opposite page, from the left:
Willie Rigney, USA
"Triumph", '90s
Made after drawings and design by W. W. Cronk. Ivory handle.
Overall length 14" (336 mm).
"Excalibur", '90s
Made after drawings and design by W. W. Cronk. Fossilzed ivory handle.
Overall length 17" (432 mm).

Opposite page, from the left:
W. W. Cronk, USA
"War Axes", early '80s
"Bat Ax", rosewood handle,
Overall length 36" (914 mm).
"Camelot", ivory handle,
Overall length 37" (940 mm). *"Brave
Heart"*, ebony wood handle.
Overall length 35" (889 mm).

On the right:
W. W. Cronk, USA
"Silent Arrows", early '80s
Made of 440C stainless steel. Ivory
handle with black ebony wood
diamond shaped insert.
Overall length 14" (336 mm).

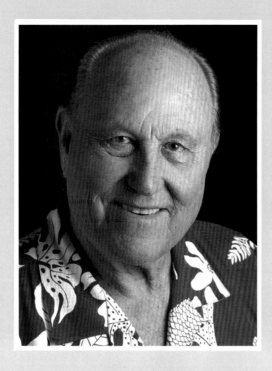

Walter Hoffman USA

Opposite page, from the left:
Henry H. Frank, USA
"Gold Folding Daggers"
Black buffalo horn handle dagger (1999), Blade length 2 5/8" (67 mm). Ivory handle folding dagger (1998), Blade length 3 1/4" (82 mm). "Big Frank" ivory handle folding dagger, used for the cover illustration on the 1999 AKI Show magazine. Blade length 3" (76 mm). All three knives have blade, bolsters, back spring and pins made of 14k hardened gold.

I have surfed giant waves at Makaha in Hawaii. I have free-dived to over 100 feet looking for record game fish. I have raced motorcycles across the California, Nevada and Mexican deserts. Nothing has given me greater pleasure and satisfaction than collecting knives. I have been collecting knives since 1983. I got into knife collecting as a diversion to my international textile business, and I now have over 300 knives and am continually upgrading my collection. On a trip to the Orient, I was exposed to a beautiful knife collection that belonged to one of my customers. As he explained the intricacies of forged steel, engraving and utility, I was spellbound. I purchased my first knife from Fred Carter and had to wait for 3 years to take delivery. If nothing else, I learned that quality isn't cheap and is worth waiting for. What started as a hobby has grown into an obsession. I love knives, their look, their feel and the skill that goes into their making. Each knife is unique, one of a kind, and contains the signature of its maker. I can tell without much inspection who made the knife, who engraved it and when it was made. I continue to be enthralled with the entire knife world and am constantly learning more and more about this ancient process. *www.hoffmanknives.com*

This page, from the top:
Wolfgang Loerchner, Canada
"Folding Persian", 2005
Carved 3 1/2" (89 mm) blade and
carved steel handle with Black-lip
pearl and Damascus inlays.
"Folding Dagger", 2003
Carved 3 1/8" (79 mm) blade and
carved steel handle with Black-lip
pearl and Damascus inlays.

Opposite page, from the top:
Ron Lake, USA
"Back Lock", 1993
Mother-of-Pearl interframe,
engraved by Ron Skaggs (USA).
Blade length 3 1/4" (82 mm).
"Dagger", 1993
Mother-of-Pearl interframe,
engraved by Ron Skaggs (USA).
Blade length 3 1/4" (82 mm).
"Nightmares In The Sky", 1994
Mother-of-Pearl interframe, gold inlaid
and engraved by John Robyn (USA).
Blade length 2 5/8" (67 mm).
"Boot Knife", 2000
Black cape buffalo handle. Boot
Blade length 3 1/4" (82 mm).
"Gold Interframe", 2001
Black-lip pearl interframe with 18k
gold handle.
Blade length 2 3/4" (70 mm).
"Gold Interframe", 2000
Black-lip pearl interframe with 18k
gold handle.
Blade length 2" (51 mm).

This page, from the top:
Joe Kious, USA
"Barth Vador", 2004
Automatic dagger engraved by Ron
Skaggs (USA). Damascus
Blade length 4" (102 mm).
"Wings of Dreams", 2005
Automatic Persian with Black-lip
pearl handle. engraved by Ron
Skaggs (USA). Damascus
Blade length 3 1/2" (89 mm).
"Dragon", 2005
Automatic Persian with Black-lip
pearl handle. engraved by Ron
Skaggs (USA). Damascus
Blade length 3" (76 mm).

Opposite page, from the left:
Joe Kious, USA
"Geisha/Samurai", 2004
Automatic, pocket locket series. Gold
inlaid and engraved by Ron Skaggs
(USA). Black-lip pearl inlay.
Blade length 3 5/8" (92 mm).
"Viking", 2005
Automatic, pocket locket series. Gold
inlaid and engraved by Ron Skaggs
(USA). Black-lip pearl inlay.
Blade length 3 3/8" (86 mm).

This page, from the top:
Reinhard Tschager, Italy
"Bachus", 2001
Full Integral knife. Black-lip pearl
handle with engraved grape vines
surrounding a carved gold head of
Bachus with diamonds for eyes.
Overall length 8 1/2" (216 mm).
Dietmar F. Kressler, Germany
"Grape Vines", 2000
Full Integral knife engraved by
M. Fleischer. Elephant ivory handle.
Overall length 8 1/4" (210 mm).
Frans Van Eldik, Holland
"Tiger Girl", 2001
Full Integral knife engraved by
D. Matagne. Blue mammoth ivory
handle.
Overall length 9 1/4" (235 mm).

Opposite page, from the top:
Bob Loveless, USA
"Matching Set Sub-Hilts", 2002
All four sub-hilt knives with black
micarta handles and marked on the
ricasso with the collector's initials
"W. H." and numbered 1-4. "Big
Bear" Overall length 8 1/2" (216 mm).
"Middle Bear" Overall length 7 1/2"
(190 mm). "Small Bear" Overall length
6 1/2" (165 mm) and "Baby Bear"
Overall length 5 1/2" (140 mm).

This page, from the top:
Bill Moran, USA
"ST-23 Fighter", 1990
Curly maple handle and sheath with silver wire inlays. All Damascus blade and fittings.
Overall length 13" (330 mm).
Buster Warenski, USA
"California Gold", 1995
Gold wrap handle, guard and sheath. Gold quartz inlays. Engraved by Julie Warenski. Made for the Art Knife Invitational show.
Overall length 12 1/4" (311 mm).

Opposite page, from the top:
Jim Schmidt, USA
"Baby Blue", 1996
Blue mastodon ivory handle with gold pins. Damascus blade and front and rear bolsters. Gold Bail.
Blade length 2 1/2" (63 mm).
"White Heart", 1995
Elephant ivory handle with gold pins. Damascus blade and front and rear bolsters. Gold Bail.
Blade length 3 1/4" (83 mm).
"After Glow", 1997
Gold-lip pearl handle with gold pins. Damascus blade, clamshell lock release and front and rear bolsters. Made for the Art Knife Invitational show.
Blade length 4" (102 mm).
"Gypsy Wish", 1999
Carved paua shell handle with gold pins. Damascus blade and gold clamshell lock release.
Blade length 3 1/4" (83 mm).
"Twilight", 1998
Two-blade folder with a Damascus clamshell lock release. Gold pins, blade studs and bail. Triple bolsters of blackened Damascus, Black-lip pearl inlays.
Blade lengths 2 1/2" (63 mm).

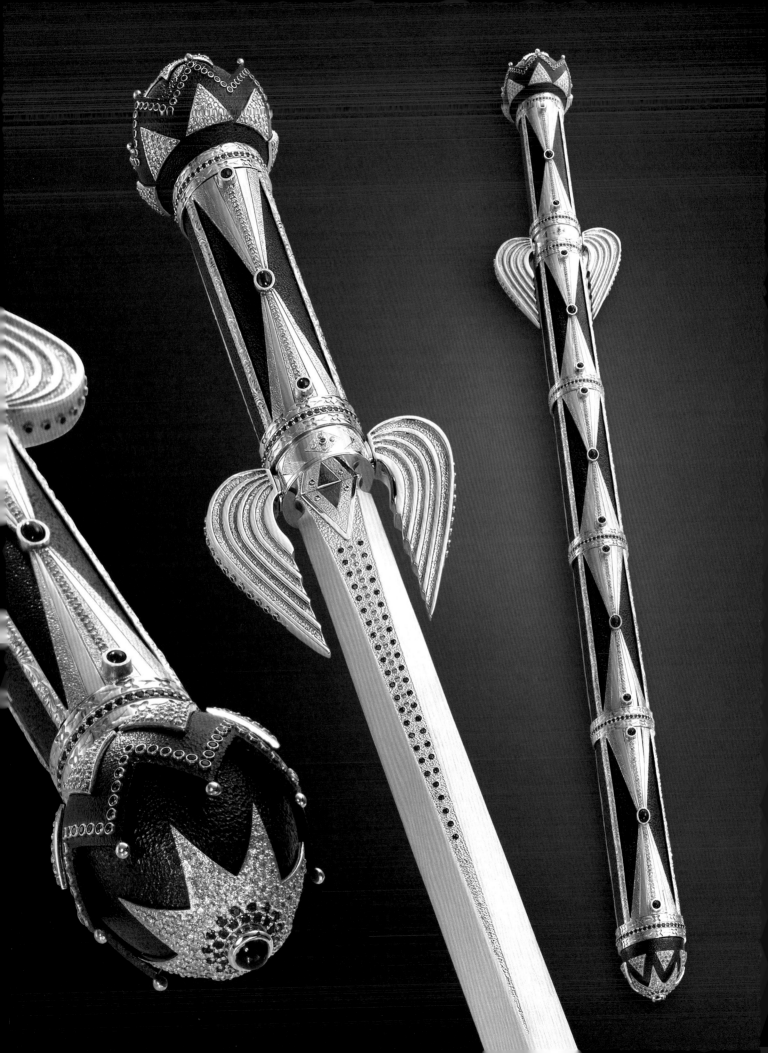

Opposite page:
Dellana and Van Barnett, USA
"Golden Heart", 2006
This majestic piece was commissioned
by Gerald Hopkin after its concept
drawing was presented to him.
It then became a collaboration
between Van Barnett, Dellana, and
Gerald Hopkin, that would become
a Scepter along with its stand and
accoutrements, designed to be an
artistic interpretation of the Royal
Scepter and Regalia. "Golden Heart"
was born as a vision of what could
be done with a knife to make it more
than just an art knife, but to try and
separate the two so as to be accepted
both as a form of art and a knife,
depending only on how one views it.
"Golden Heart" is the first in
a new collaborative series between
Van Barnett and Dellana. These knives
will be called the "Majesty" series,
with strong emphasis on art, beauty
and illusion. These collaborative
efforts are created under the name
"VALANI" ™, combining the names of
both artists.
Four years in the making, this Scepter
(symbol of imperial authority) has an
18" (457 mm) solid 14k yellow spring
gold blade, with diamonds and rubies.
Sheath and handle are constructed
of oxidized, textured sterling silver
tubing and solid 14k yellow gold
set with diamonds, facetted rubies,
cabochon rubies and hand engraving.
Altogether there are 786 Rubies
(53.2 carats) and over 855 diamonds
(20.35 carats), 2.69 pounds (1.22
kg) of sterling silver, 4.173 pounds
(1.892 kg) of 14k yellow gold. Overall
sheathed length 26 1/2" (673 mm).

Gerald Hopkin Barbados

I have been collecting art knives for a relatively short period of time in
comparison to other major collectors. However, my taste in art knives varies
almost right across the board, in that I collect anything I deem to be art.
Great art knives are born of an unusual design entailing the distinctive
use of rare, precious and semi-precious materials. In almost all cases,
they require anywhere from three months to two years to complete. My
background in building very high-end residences has given me a salient
advantage when it comes to deciding what works and what does not in
the design process. This is directly reflected in the quality of my input and
direction when working with a knifemaker. I thoroughly enjoy this phase
where a project can sometimes take as long as two years to complete.
All correspondence with knifemakers - that is, sketches and e-mails - are
printed and filed for easy reference. My collection is not limited to just
knives (i.e., Bowies, hunters, etc.); it includes various forms of "edged art",
as can be seen in a few of the items shown in my section of this book.
"Golden Heart" displayed on the opposite page, could probably qualify
for the title of the most extraordinary and elaborate modern art knife
made to date. My knives are stored and displayed in a large safe room,
which allows me to view my entire collection very easily without having
to engage in any direct handling. Being able to readily appreciate such a
variety of overtly unique pieces in this environment is truly gratifying.

Above:

Rick Eaton, USA

"The Great Hunter", 2006

Folding side lock step-down, Persian style Fighter with a double-grind and trailing point 440C stainless steel blade. Handle is an Integral construction slab of 410 stainless steel. Full relief carving of leaves on guard and ring guard, engraved scroll leaves on back end in full relief, Banknote style leaves on blade and handle with Bulino 3D shading. Flush inlays of 24k gold on blade and handle and 24k raised gold inlays on handle. Portrait of white hunter with gun on one side with 24k gold inlays, portrait of African hunter on other side with spear. African game scenes on both sides.
Overall length 12 1/4" (311 mm).

Opposite page, from the left:

Rick Eaton, USA

"King Arthur" folders, 2001

Considered Rick Eaton's best work, these two folders, took 24 months of actual full time work to complete.
Folding Fighter: Side lock interframe, with a 440C stainless steel blade with Arabesque semi-relief engraving and 24k gold inlaid vines. Step-down Black-lip pearl and abalone mosaic

handle with full relief carving and 24k gold inlay showing King Arthur with his sword in the stone and his coronation (reverse side).
Overall length 8 3/4" (219 mm).
Persian Design: Side lock interframe, with a 440C stainless steel blade with Arabesque semi-relief engraving and 24k gold inlaid vines. Step-down Black-lip pearl and abalone mosaic handle with full relief carving of 24k gold inlay showing King Arthur going to battle and returning victorious (reverse side). This was the only folder to receive the "Cronk" award (2001 Knifemaker's Guild Show).
Overall length 10 3/5" (265 mm).

On the left:
Arpad Bojtos, Slovakia
Christopher Columbus", 2004
Stainless steel blade, deeply carved, silver fittings with 18k gold and carved mammoth ivory handle. Overall length 15" (381 mm).

Opposite page:
Larry Fuegen, USA
"Hernan Cortes, the Conquistador", 2004
This folder exhibits the wealth Cortes was able to acquire in the New World. The handle is carved mammoth ivory, with a fossil walrus ivory insert. All of the fittings, armor, cape, plumes and bolster are solid 18k gold. The helmet is white gold with pink gold trim and a yellow gold crest. The plumes are green, pink, yellow and a royal yellow gold and the cape and bolsters are yellow gold. All of the parts were made by forming sheet gold in special forms made for each piece. The 5 3/8" (136 mm) long, 270 layers Ladder pattern Damascus blade was carved and etched before it was gold plated. Overall length is 12 1/4" (311 mm)

Above:
Bruce C. Bump, USA
"Brutus", 2006
Matchlock ignition gun-axe combination. 15th century styling serpentine with gold and ruby eyes and a spring loaded jaw that clamps the slow match. Barrel is 1018, 1084, 15n20, 203e twisted canister Damascus. Axe head is 1084 and 15n20 1000 layers of random forged to shape with laddered edges, bored and breeched for key. Wood is fiddle-back maple from Chuck Bybee. Bronze furniture. Trigger is folded. Simply push the protruded portion forward and it swings down and the snake lifts its head. Gold wire inlays and engraving by Jere Davidson. Silver wire and MOP inlays in the wood by Jay Hendrickson. Blueing and color case hardening, Doug Turnbull. Serpent's design Brian Bump. Overall length 29 1/2" (749 mm).
"30 months in conceiving and making. Many of the parts were made 2 or 3 times before they fit and worked. My most challenging piece yet but I couldn't have done it without help from others on the embellishments. It was Jay Hendrickson's first ever gun silver and pearl inlays. He asked Bill Moran's advice before he started work on it and Bill said "Don't do it... just send it back". I'm glad Jay didn't take his advice".

Opposite page:
Bruce C. Bump, USA
"Love and War", 2003
A cap-lock Cook design Under-Hammer black powder caliber .22 pistol-folding knife combination. The Blade and bolsters are 3000 layer 1084/15n20/nickel Twist Damascus. Embellished with 4 mm sapphires and 14k gold studs, 14k gold plated trigger, hammer and pivot. Engraving and gold wire inlay by Jere Davidson. Blade length 4" (102 mm) and Overall length 11" (279 mm).

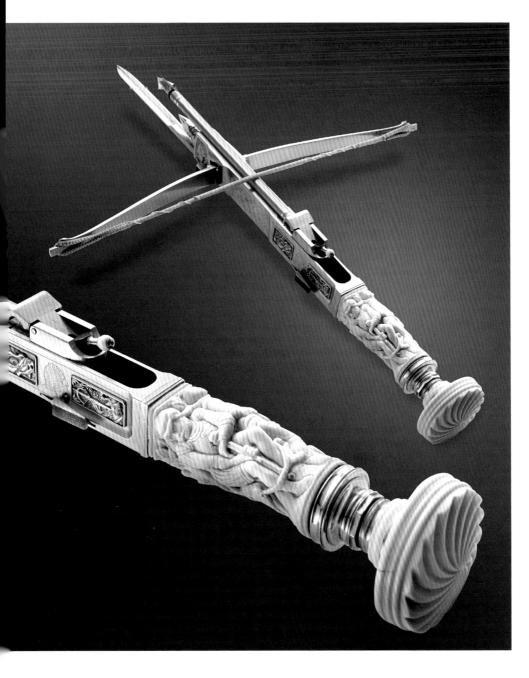

Left:
Jack Levin, USA
"Blade-Bow", 2006
This is the first known attempt
to make a working crossbow of
portable size combined with a blade,
and have both weapons perfectly
complimenting each other in
hunting. The crossbow on top has
a unique sliding-locking mechanism
allowing building up the pressure
to 150 lbs. The blade (bayonet)
opens from the bottom. 24k gold
inlays, engraving, 18k gold plates
with pictures of hunting and mystic
dragon. Handle is decorated with
carved ivory and porcelain sculptures
executed in the style of Medieval
West European paintings.
Overall length " (mm).

Opposite page:
Jack Levin, USA
"Don Quixote", 2003
A one-of-a-kind folding version
(automatic knuckle-guard) of the
medieval poniard using a unique
mechanism never repeated again.
Handle was carved from a bar of
Swedish tool steel. The blade design,
inspired by a French presentation
dagger, was carved from Swedish
Damascus and engraved by Chris
Meyer. Frame engraved by Ron Nott.
Overall length 12" (305 mm).

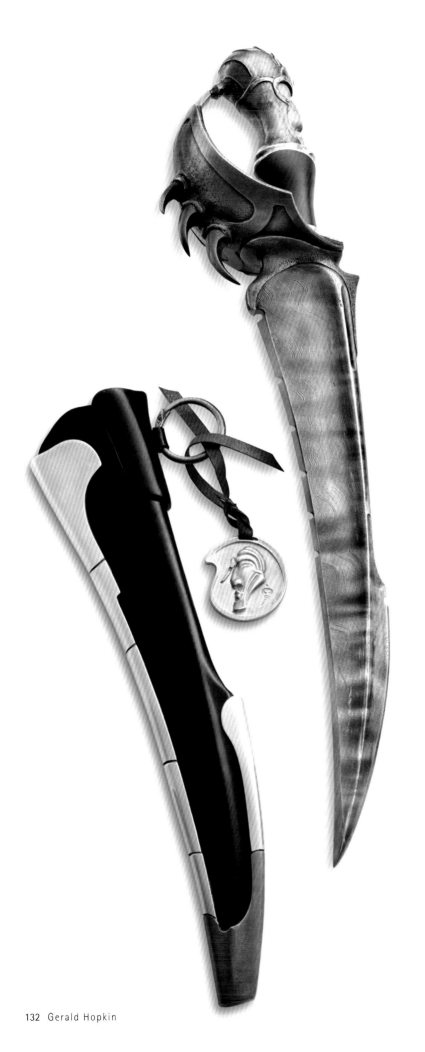

On the left:

Virgil England, Alaska

"Shi Ak Xtapos - Lord of the Watch", 2005

Chaos Fighter made of Damascus steel, silver, bronze, ivory and leather, was created, according to Virgil England, to be used in confrontations involving the Seth Daemon. The Damascus billet for the blade was forge welded by Daryl Meier then forged to shape by Virgil.
Overall length 18" (457 mm).

Opposite page:

Jose C. de Braga, Canada

"Perseus", 2004

Named after the hero who cut off Medusa's head, giving birth to Pegasus from her blood, Perseus is found in Northern Hemisphere. Perseus is a "D" guard short glaive, with a 15" (381 mm) CPM S30V steel blade. The handle is jet-stone composite with 14k gold, with oxidized sterling silver appliqués set with two large oval red garnets. On the pommel face, along with a 4 pt diamond, 14k gold pin and an 8 mm red garnet, is the 14k gold carving of the figure of Medusa. The sheath is made of tiger maple with gold furniture.
Overall length 23" (584 mm).

Above, from the left:
Roger Bergh, Sweden
"D Guard Fighter", 2004
A 5-bar blade with a gold and
diamond insert. Handle is fossil
mammoth ivory, ancient walrus
ivory, oxidized sterling silver, 18k
gold and black and white diamonds.
Tooled leather sheath with silver,
gold and ivory furniture.
Overall length 19" (483 mm).
"Orca", 2003
Sculpted Firecracker Damascus blade,
forged from 20C and 15N20 carbon
steels. Damascus bolster forged from
carbon steels. Handle is sculpted
stabilized masur birch, fossil walrus
ivory, fossil mammoth ivory and 18k
gold detailing.
Overall length 13 1/4" (336 mm).

Opposite page, from the left:
Ron Best, USA
"Tanto" and "Wakisashi" (2004),
"Fighter", (2005)
Three Full Integrals, each of them
carved from single pieces of D2
steel, including the two sheaths for
the Wakisashi and the Tanto. The
Wakisashi and the Fighter started off
as two 20 lb. blocks of D2 steel! The
Wakisashi has a 16" (406 mm) blade
and Overall length of 24 1/2" (622
mm). The Tanto has a 12" (305 mm)
blade and an Overall length of 17 3/4"
(451 mm). The Integral Fighter has
an 11" (279 mm) blade, with pre-ban
elephant ivory for the handle. Sheath
is maple with stainless steel and pre-
ban elephant ivory furniture.
Overall length 17 1/2" (444 mm).

On the left:

Zaza Revishvili, USA

"Cross guard Dagger", 2003

Designing this piece was inspired by Italian daggers carried by royalty during the Renaissance Period. These were elegant, elaborate and symmetrical long daggers of similar dimensions. Zaza's design is enriched with filigree and the touches of color from natural A grade garnets. The Devin Thomas stainless steel Tie-twist pattern Damascus used for the blade, harmonizes with the texture of the handle and sheath.
Overall length 24" (610 mm).

Opposite page:

Doug Casteel, USA

"D-guard Kurki", 2006

An old knife pattern with a touch of the 20th century, this outstanding Kukri was made by Doug Casteel using Mike Norris stainless Damascus. The 14" (356 mm) Ladder pattern Damascus blade was flat ground with a top clip that is also edged. All remaining metal was crafted from aluminum-bronze using heat to move and bring it to shape. The bronze was then carved and the background removed giving it the required depth.
Overall length 19 1/2" (495 mm).
Photography: Daniel Christaldi

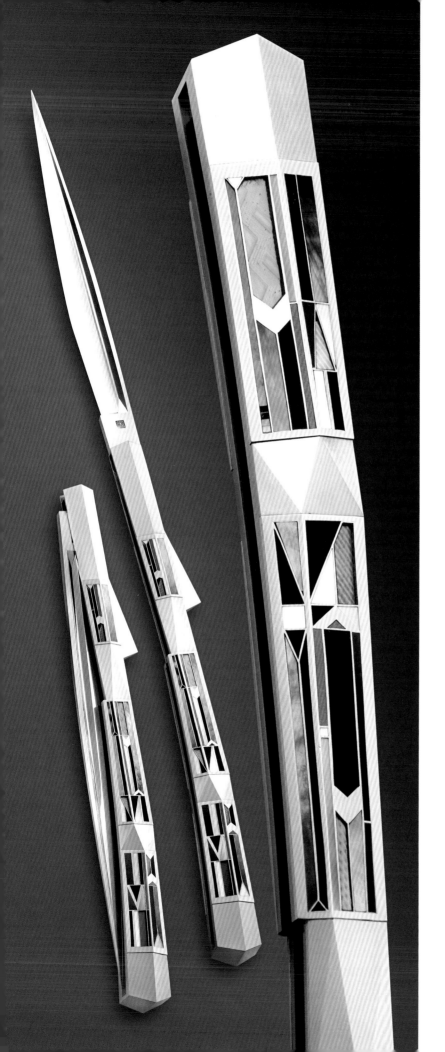

On the left:

Jurgen Steinau, Germany

"No. 06 07 20.4", 2006

Lockback folder with an RWL 34 blade. Stainless steel handle and 18k gold inserts inlaid with Black-lip pearl, Mother-of-Pearl, various stones and bakelite.
Overall length 14" (356 mm).

Paul Jarvis, USA

"Genghis Khan", 2006

This knife was eight months in the making. The 15 3/4" (400 mm) blade is carved and pierced Daryl Meier Damascus. Habaki is carved and pierced sterling silver. Handle and Fittings are mammoth ivory, carved sterling silver in high relief bamboo design with 24k gold inlays, 14k gold hand carved insects and 9 emeralds and 8 rubies set in 14k gold bezels.
Overall length 21" (533 mm),

Thomas C. Hutton *USA*

My knife collecting began in 1980 with the purchase of an old, tattered, 1970s *Blade Magazine* that I found at a flea market in Reno, Nevada (USA). As I looked through the magazine, I was instantly hooked. The beauty and craftsmanship of the knives was like nothing I had ever seen before. I promptly ordered brochures from the knifemakers whose work impressed me most. My first purchase was a Tommy Lee Boot-knife with a delivery date a year away. Since the collecting itch had already started to take hold, I couldn't wait that long. I discovered a knife show that was being held in Glendale, California, and purchased (cash and carry) a Butch Beaver boot-knife. It was beautiful. Shortly thereafter, I attended the 1983 Guild Show in Kansas City, Missouri. There, in one room, were all the knife makers from the magazine (and more) displaying their wares. I've been collecting custom made knives ever since. I show and trade knives at the Antique Arms and Knife Show in Las Vegas, NV and at the Solvang Knife Show held in California.

This page, from the top:
Ron Richard, USA
"Ron Richard has been making knives since 1968. He worked under Bob Hayes early on in his career. A key design element of his folding knives is that they all have dead bolt button locks".
"Richard's Dead Bolt Button Lock", early '80s
Interframe, antique tortoise shell insets.
Overall length 5" (127 mm).
"Richard's Dead Bolt Button Lock", early '80s
Interframe, ivory handle.
Overall length 5" (127 mm).

Opposite page, from the top:
Jim Schmidt, USA
"Sea Flyer", 1985
Antique tortoise shell inlay, Damascus frame and blade. Stainless steel liner with filework.
Overall length 9 1/4" (235 cm).
"Fish Breath", 1988
Damascus blade and bolsters, chocolate mastodon ivory handle. Stainless steel liner and filework.
Overall length 9 1/2" (241 mm).
"Pocket Posie", 1990
Damascus bolsters, blade and back spring. Stag handle. File worked stainless steel liners.
Overall length 6" (152 mm).
"Caron", 1984
Damascus blade and bolsters. Stainless steel liners with file work. Ivory handle.
Overall length 9" (229 mm).
"No Sweat", 2001
Folding fighter with Damascus and blade and bolsters and gold pins. Stainless steel liner with file work. Ivory handle.
Overall length 9 1/2" (241 mm).

This page, from the left:

Michael Walker, USA

"Liner Lock", early '90s
Color anodized titanium frame, engraved in color by Pat Walker. Overall length 6 1/2" (165 mm).

"Liner Lock", late '80s
Sterling silver frame. Anodized titanium liners, bolster and clip. Overall length 6 3/4" (171 mm).

"D-Lock", late '90s
Titanium frame with Damascus inlay and gold inlays. Damascus blade with gold inlays. Overall length 7 1/4" (184 mm).

"D-Lock", 2002
Titanium frame and Damascus scales. D-lock stainless steel button. Overall length 6 3/4" (171 mm).

Opposite page, from the top:

Jim Schmidt, USA

"Rodtie Root Boot", 1992
Folding boot knife with Damascus blade and bolsters. Stainless steel liner with filework. Mother-of-Pearl handle. Overall length 9 1/8" (232 mm).

"Wind Whispers", 1993
Damascus blade and bolsters. Gold pins. Stainless steel liner with filework. Mother-of-Pearl handle. Overall length 9 1/2" (241 mm).

"Shimmer", 1986
Damascus blade and bolsters. Gold pins. Filework on top of blade. Mother-of-Pearl handle. Overall length 8 1/4" (210 mm).

"Nik-Nac", 1991
Damascus blade and bolsters. Filework on top of blade. Stainless steel liners with filework. Black-lip pearl handle. Overall length 7 1/4" (184 mm).

"Humming Bird", 2000
Wharncliffe Damascus blade and Damascus bolsters. Black-lip pearl handle. Rose gold liners with filework and rose gold pins. Overall length 4 5/8" (117 mm).

Opposite page, from top left
to lower right:

Virgil England, USA
"Shantu Princess", late '90s
Damascus steel, bronze, mammoth
ivory. Scrimshaw by Virgil England.
Overall length 2" (51 mm).

"The Fool", mid '90s
Damascus steel, silver, bronze,
mammoth ivory broach. Scrimshaw
by Virgil England.
Overall length 3 1/4" (82 mm).

"The Worm Lord", 1996
Damascus steel, silver, bronze,
mammoth ivory broach. Scrimshaw
by Virgil England.
Overall length 2 5/8" (67 mm).

"Ice Hunter", 2001
Damascus steel, silver, bronze, ancient
walrus ivory, red lace, leather.
Overall length 5 1/2" (140 mm).

"Ko Ak Sha Bu", 2001
Damascus steel, 22k gold, rubies,
silver, mammoth ivory, leather
pendant/broach.
Overall length 2 5/8" (67 mm).

On the right:
Jim Ence, USA
"Knife and Fork Set", mid '80s
4-piece 440C stainless steel set
of knife, fork, spoon, and ivory
toothpick. Fluted ivory handle with
silver wire wrap.

Bob Loveless, USA
"Riverside Boot", late '80s
Nickel-silver hilt. Brown micarta handle with red liners.
Overall length 9 3/4" (248 mm).
"Riverside Boot", late '80s
Hilt engraved in gold by Dan Wilkerson. Stag handles with
red liners.
Overall length 9 1/4" (235 mm).
"Riverside Skinner", 1990
Nickel-silver hilt. Stag handles with red liners.
Overall length 8 1/4" (235 mm).
"Riverside Neismuk", early '80s
Nickel-silver hilt. Dark maroon micarta handles with red liners.
Overall length 9 1/2" (241 mm).

Opposite page, from the top:
Steve R. Johnson, USA
"Skinner", early 2000's
ATS 34 steel blade. Stag handle with
red liners.
Overall length 9 1/8" (232 mm).
"Skinner", mid '90s
ATS 34 steel blade. Woolly mammoth
handle with red liners.
Overall length 9" (229 mm).
"Skinner", mid '90s
ATS 34 steel blade. Mastadon ivory
handle with red liners.
Overall length 8 1/8 (206 mm).
"Skinner", mid '90s
ATS 34 steel blade. Stag handle with
red liners.
Overall length 9" (229 mm).

Photo: Tim Berberich

Frozen Matanuska River, Alaska, December 2006

William J. Jury and William J. Jury III Alaska

Opposite page, from the left
Zaza Revishvili, USA
"Persian Princess", 2005
A letter opener with stainless Damascus blade. Sheath and handle in fine filigree technique. Stones are natural garnets.
Overall length 8" (203 mm).
"Vendetta", 2005
Zaza's own designed series, "Count Monte Christo". Mike Norris stainless steel Blade. Bolsters are carbon steel Robert Eggerling Mosaic Damascus. Handle executed in fine filigree technique. Stones are blue sapphire and black onyx.
Overall length 10 9/16" (268 mm).
"The Tsar's Dagger", 1995
Zaza's own design reflecting traditional characteristics. Carbon steel Mosaic Damascus blade forged by Owen Wood. The handle and sheath executed in fine filigree technique. Stones are top quality natural garnets.
Overall length 17 1/8" (435 mm).

William Jury was born in Fairbanks, Alaska, in 1945. His father was a railroad engineer, so he lived in many small remote areas along the Alaska Railroad. Fishing and hunting were the way of life for William as he grew up. He appreciated all of the opportunities that Alaska had to offer. When his father retired from the Alaska Railroad, William and his family moved to Oregon, where he completed his high school studies. The day after graduation William returned to Alaska. Shortly after entering the work force, William was drafted into the military and served in Southeast Asia. William Jury III was born in 1968, ten days before William Sr. completed his tour of duty. William Jr. graduated from High School in 1987 and later received his B.A. from Seattle Pacific University and his Masters Degree from San Francisco State University. While attending a gun show in Las Vegas, William Jr. convinced his father to visit a knife show that was also taking place in Las Vegas. It was at this time that two instant knife collectors were born. Both William and William Jr. began collecting in 2005. They find custom knives to be wonderful objects of art, and appreciate the talent and the diversity of the artists who create them.

This page, from the top:

Dellana, USA

"Mini Bling", 2006

Lockback Folder #81. Composite Damascus blade forged by Dellana with a center composite wedge of W-2 carbon steel selectively etched in a circle pattern. Sterling silver handle overlaid with engraved and textured 14k yellow gold inlaid with numerous diamonds. Presentation grade Mother-of-Pearl file worked and inlaid with numerous diamonds set in 14k yellow gold and 14k gold dots. 14k yellow gold lock release with diamonds. Altogether 57 diamonds totaling 1.86 carats. Overall length 7" (178 mm).

"Yes", 2006

Lockback Folder #79. Ladder pattern Damascus blade made by Dellana. 14k polished yellow gold thumbstud with diamond. 14k yellow gold engraved and textured handle with presentation grade Mother-of-Pearl. Rubies set in hand fabricated 24k gold and 14k yellow gold overlaid surface embellishments - some dots and some textured solid 14k sheet. Inlaid diamonds set in 14k yellow gold. File worked all over.
Overall length 6 1/2" (165 mm).

"Jewelie", 1994

Lock back Folder #4, the 4th knife Dellana ever made! W-2 carbon steel forged Blade by Dellana (the only knife she made with a plain steel blade). The first 18k gold "Dellana Dots" Dellana ever made. Amethyst pyramid cabochons set in 14k yellow gold. Sterling silver filed and sanded to shape handle with presentation grade Brown-lip pearl. Lock release with pyramid garnets set in fabricated 14k yellow gold settings and riveted to the lock bar. Fully file worked in and out. Overall length 5 1/8" (130 mm).

Opposite page, from the left:

Van Barnett, USA

"Bill's Dagger", 2006

Fluted ebony handle. 14k gold fittings and carved Damascus guard and pommel with 24k gold wash. Carved W2 and 203-e Damascus blade. Overall length 12 1/2" (317 mm).

"Living proof", 1997

Ladder pattern Rosebud Damascus by Van Barnett, Nitre blued. Carved and hot blued fittings. Carved fossil walrus ivory handle and carved roses. 14k gold fittings and 12 diamonds set in the handle and guard.
Overall length 19 1/4" (489 mm).

Opposite page, from the right:

Stephen Olszewski, USA

"Bali #1", 2006

Stephen's first Balisong. Blade steel by Larry Donnelley, bolsters are Rados Turkish Damascus, scales are premium Black-lip pearl. File worked and anodized titanium liners. Back bars carved with oak leaf motifs and gold inlays to match. Fully carved bolsters with raised oak leaf motifs and background deeply etched to show the Damascus pattern. The handles were made 3/4" longer than usual to provide enough weight for easy flipping. Overall length 10 1/2" (267 mm).

"Oak leaf Auto", 2005

A latch released liner lock auto. Blade forged to shape from Rados Turkish Damascus. Bolsters are Rados Turkish Damascus with deep relief carving of acorn and oak leaf motifs. Premium Black-lip pearl scales. Overall length 10 1/16" (256 mm).

"Crusader Auto", 2005

Forged to shape Rados Turkish Damascus blade. Bolsters are Rados Ladder pattern Damascus. The front bolsters with cross pattern and rear bolsters carved with lion's head, hot blued brown and blue. Premium walrus scales. Overall length 9 3/16" (233 mm).

"Lizard auto", 2001

A "figural" knife. Blade steel is Eggerling Snakeskin pattern Damascus, bolsters are Eggerling Turkish Damascus, hot blued brown hues to compliment the mammoth ivory scales. Latch is hidden in a leg and the screws become eyes. Overall length 9 9/16" (243 mm).

Right:

Harry Leo Smith, USA

"Dream Keeper", 2005

One year in the making. Blade is 4 5/16" (110 mm) long 440 stainless steel worked to look like napped flint with serrated edges. Carved ivory handle with bronze figure head, surrounded by abalone. Sheath is hand carved fossilized walrus ivory.

Above, from the left:

Ernest R. Emerson, USA

"Commander GMAN", 2005

Emerson/Pennington collaboration Commander prototype.
Overall length 8 13/16" (224 mm).

"Tactical Persian", 2006

A folding version of the fixed-blade knife Emerson made for operators deployed in Bosnia in the '90s. It features a graceful upswept blade and a delicate point. Overall length 9 1/2" (241 mm).

"Full Dress CQC-6", '90s

One of the most sought after custom knives in custom knife collecting and is bought and tested like a commodity all over the world. Devin Thomas Ladder pattern Damascus chisel ground Tanto blade. Overall length 8 1/8" (206 mm).

"Full Dress CQC-6", '90s

A modified version of Emerson's CQC-6 design, made to commemorate a trip to the cutlery festival in Seki City, Japan. It features a drop point design, not a Tanto since Tanto style knives were illegal to sell or own in Japan. Pearl handles, satin finished bolsters. Overall length 8 1/16" (204 mm).

Opposite page, from the top:

Bob Lum, USA

Snakewood Stalker, 2006

Blade with sharpened swedge, snakewood handle.
Overall length 10 1/8" (256 mm).

"Tanto", 2006

Fossilized walrus ivory handle.
Overall length 10 9/16" (268 mm).

"All Ti Folding Stalker", 2006

Michael Walker locking mechanism, titanium handle.
Overall length 11 1/8" (282 mm).

"All Ti Forester", 2006

Frame lock folder, titanium handle.
Overall length 9 13/16" (249 mm).

"Chinese Folder", 2006

Chinese folder with a drilled titanium handle.
Overall length 9 1/16" (230 mm).

"Left Handed Forester", 2006

All titanium left handed liner lock.
Overall length 8 1/2" (216 mm).

This page, from the top:

Richard Wright, USA

"Ambidextrous Bolster Release Double Bladed Switchblade (No. 105)", 2005

The large blade is step ground in a dagger design, the smaller blade is designed as a "skull crusher". Both blades are Devin Thomas Basket Weave stainless Damascus. Bolsters are a composite of sterling silver and Devin Thomas Damascus. Black-lip pearl scales with solid gold screws.
Overall length 13 1/4" (336 mm).

"Ambidextrous Bolster Release Switchblade (No. 97)", 2004

Celtic dagger design. The blade is forged to shape from Rados Turkish Twist Damascus. The front bolsters are a composite of Rados Damascus with sterling silver cross guards carved to shape in a basic Celtic knot design.
Overall length is 11 7/8" (302 mm).

"Ambidextrous Bolster Release Switchblade (No. 95)", 2004

Clip point blade forged to shape from Rados Turkish Twist Damascus. Front and rear bolsters are made from an Ithaca 10ga. Damascus shotgun barrel. Knife design is based on a Spanish "Navajo" knife. Scales are fossil walrus ivory.
Overall length 12 1/2" (317 mm).

Opposite page, from the left:

Larry Fuegen, USA

"Balisong", 2006

The 1095 carbon steel blade is hand forged, carved and hand rubbed to a satin finish. Hand carved and polished steel bolsters and hand carved Mother-of-Pearl handle scales. Stainless steel liners are fully file worked. Carved steel spacer, file worked and overlaid with solid 18k yellow gold on the outside. *"According to Larry, making this Bali opened for him a whole new dimension in knifemaking".*
Overall length 10 1/4" (260 mm).

Chuck Gedraitis, USA

"Bali Number 24", 2006

Mokume bolsters and Damascus blade.
Overall length 10" (254 mm).

Charles Marlowe, USA

"Damasteel SOS Bali", 2006

Blade steel is 20-turn twist Damasteel, hardware is all stainless steel. Features the IKBS (Ikoma Korth bearing system). Latch and spacers are made from same Damascus.
Overall length 9 1/16" (230 mm).

Audra Draper, USA

"Bali #8", 2005

Blade is 15N20 and 1084 Damascus of a Twisted Pattern. The handles are solid brass, milled to fit the blade, and the washers. Overall length 8 1/2" (216 mm).

Koji Hara, Japan, *2006*

Bowie shaped blade and wooden handles carved to resemble bamboo. Overall length 11 1/2" (292 mm).

Buster Warenski, USA
"King Tut Dagger", 1987

Buster Warenski s "King Tut Dagger" is a faithful solid gold reproduction of the solid gold knife found with the 3,300-year-old mummy of the Egyptian pharaoh Tutankhamen. This project, conceived in the early 1980s, helped spearhead the contemporary art knife renaissance. The first knife in Warenski s Legacy Series, it is entirely made of 18k gold and 24k gold.
A picture of the King Tut dagger was used on the cover of the 1993 AKI catalog and its outline embossed on the 1983 and 1984 covers.

"After 4 years of experimenting and learning, I was able to complete the project. Some of the difficult techniques used here were granulation and cloisonn. Casting the blade was also a real challenge, as it required pouring nearly 10 oz. of 18k gold. After several failures, I was able to make the casting by first making a steel mold. This is by far the most complicated project I have ever done".
Overall length 12 1/2" (317 mm).

Phil Lobred USA

I have collected knives since I was about ten years old and started collecting custom knives in 1968. I attended my first Knifemaker's Guild show and was made an honorary member in 1972. In 1973, Gil Hibben set up his shop in my garage in Anchorage, Alaska, and I learned the knife business from the inside out. The inspiration for both the Art Knife Invitational and the King Tut dagger developed around 1980, and I produced the first AKI Show in 1983. The King Tut dagger became a reality in 1986. I have changed directions several times over the years but have collected mainly 1850 San Francisco style knives for the last 20 years, including several, very rare, antique, California knives from this period. I do still enjoy any fine custom knife and add an occasional Damascus folder or ivory handled, drop point hunter to my collection. Over the last few years I have limited my collecting to the work of a selected group of knifemakers.

Above:
Michael Walker, USA
Sharkstooth zipper, 1997
Blade lock with a composite blade
of titanium and stainless Damascus.
Stainless Damascus frame with
Mother-of-Pearl, titanium, Meteorite,
silver and gold.
Overall length 7 5/8" (194 mm).

Opposite page, from the left:
Herman Schneider, USA, *1977*
Ivory handle and stainless steel
bolsters. Engraved by Lynton McKenzie,
scrimshaw by Adam Funmaker.
Blade length 3 1/8" (79 mm).
Buster Warenski, USA, *1978*
Ivory handle and nickel-silver bolsters.
Engraved by Lynton McKenzie,
scrimshaw by Buster Warenski.
Blade length 3 1/8" (79 mm).

Opposite page, from the left:
Herman Schneider, USA
"Push Dagger", 1981
Whale s tooth handle, ebony fitting,
stainless steel sheath.
Blade length 4 1/8" (105 mm).
"Dirk", 1980
Gold bolsters and escutcheon,
Mother-of-Pearl handle. Engraved by
Lynton McKenzie.
Blade length 3 7/8" (98 mm).
Michael Collins, USA
"Push-Dagger" and "Dirk", 1980
Stainless steel fittings, ivory handles.
Engraved by Michael Collins.
Blade lengths: Push-dagger 4 1/8"
(105 mm), Dirk 4 7/8" (124 mm).

Above:
James Schmidt, USA
"Lanyard lock", 1999
Lanyard lock, Ladder pattern Schmidt
Damascus and Damascus bolsters.
Silver frame, fossil walrus ivory handle
scales, file worked and a gold bail.
Overall length 7 1/2" (190 mm).

Left, from the top:
Contemporary San Francisco Knives
Buster Warenski, USA, *1999*
Mammoth ivory handle, gold fittings, gold tang wrap, silver sheath with gold throat.
Engraved by Julie Warenski.
Blade length 7" (178 mm).
Buster Warenski, *1995*
Gold wrap, gold fittings, Mother-of-Pearl inlay, 20 diamond studs, gold sheath. Engraved by Julie Warenski.
Blade length 6 5/8" (168 mm).
Buster Warenski, *1980*
Silver fittings, mammoth ivory handle, silver sheath. Carved and engraved by Buster Warenski.
Blade length 6 1/8" (156 mm).

Opposite page, from the left:
Contemporary San Francisco Knives
Buster Warenski, USA, *2002*
Silver wrapped with silver fittings and African sugilite inlays and silver sheath with sugilite.
Engraved by Julie Warenski.
Blade length 5 3/4" (mm).
Buster Warenski, *1999*
Gold wrap, gold hilt and fittings, gold-quartz inlays, silver sheath with gold throat and tip and gold-quartz escutcheon.
Engraved by Julie Warenski.
Blade length 6 5/8" (168 mm).
Buster Warenski, *1994*
Abalone, Mother-of-Pearl and silver inlays, silver fittings, gold inlays, silver sheath. Engraved by Julie Warenski.
Blade length 6 1/4" (159 mm).
Buster Warenski, *2001*
Gold wrap and hilt, gold-quartz and jasper inlays, silver sheath with gold throat and tip, and a gold-quartz frog button. Engraved by Julie Warenski.
Blade length 6" (152 mm).

This page, from the right:
Contemporary San Francisco Knives
Jim Ence, USA, *1994*
Silver wrap, gold fittings, 20 ruby
studs, fossil walrus ivory inlay, silver
sheath. Engraved by Julie Warenski.
Blade length 6 1/8" (156 mm).
Jim Hardenbrook, USA, *1983*
Silver fittings, fossil walrus ivory
handle, gold inlays, silver sheath.
Engraved by Ron Skaggs.
Blade length 6 1/8" (156 mm).
Ted Dowell, USA, *1991*
Integral construction. Engraved and
carved blued steel inlay by Julie
Warenski. Ebony sheath.
Blade length 5" (127 mm).

Opposite page, from the left:
San Francisco Style Dress Knives
All four knives have mosaic inlayed
handles made of gold bearing quartz.
All are gold wrapped with gold
hilts and silver sheaths. All were
engraved by Julie Warenski.
Steven Rapp, USA, *2004*
Will & Finck 1850 style dress Bowie
with 5 7/8" (149 mm) blade.
Steven Rapp, USA, *2002*
Michael Price style dress Bowie with
5" (127 mm) blade.
Steven Rapp, USA, *1999*
Double edged, Michael Price style
dress knife with 6" (152 mm) blade.
Steven Rapp, USA, *2000*
Michael Price 1850 style dress bowie
with a 5 3/4" (146 mm) blade.

Marlene and Dr. Laurence Marton

Dr. Laurence J. Marton *USA*

Opposite page, from the left:
James Schmidt, USA, *1983*
Boot knife, Damascus blade, Damascus
and ebony handle and sheath.
Overall length 8 1/8" (206 mm).
*"This is the knife that Nate Posner
chose to withhold from us (see
chapter on Marlene's knives), forcing
us to attend the Solvang Show
and indoctrinating us into knife
collecting. Obviously, in time, we
convinced him to let us care for it!"*
Rob Hudson, USA, *1995*
and Jim Kelso, USA, *1997*
Persian style dagger, 7-bar
composite Damascus blade, carved
ebony, engraved and pierced silver,
gold and opal handle.
Overall length 20 3/4" (527 mm).
Kaj Embretsen, Sweden, *1999*
Viking dress dagger, multi-bar
Damascus blade, ironwood and
Damascus handle.
Overall length 11 5/16" (287 mm).
*"This dagger was shown to me by
Jim Schmidt as an example of a knife
that Jim thought only 2 or 3 people in
the world could execute".*

The genesis of my knife collecting is described in detail in David Darom's chapter on my wife's collection. The joy of having your wife ignite a silent passion that transforms itself into a flaming reality cannot be minimized, and the fact that this "insanity" is now shared by us both is wondrous. While this collection clearly reflects our tastes, a fundamental principle of ours is to stimulate knifemakers to take the next step in their evolving creativity. As such, while we have frequently made gentle suggestions, the final creative product reflects the individual knifemaker or, in some instances, collaborative genius. We enjoy telling the myriad stories behind our knives, understanding the responsibility of conveying the artistic passions of each knife's creator. Each knife represents a segment of the knifemaker's life, a snapshot of the creative process that evolves over many years. We will highlight just a few of the wonderful knives shown here (many other knives from this collection have already appeared in earlier volumes by David Darom). The Jambiya that graced Buster Warenski's home page on his website represents his (and Julie's) remarkably unique abilities and desire to go beyond the norm. Fred Carter's very first all steel dagger evoked passion and frustration during its creation, and was actually lost in the US mail for quite some time before it arrived. The collaboration between Rob Hudson and Jim Kelso represents Rob's return to knifemaking after a very serious accident, and the first collaboration between these two unique artists. The Michael Walker – Merry Lee Rae folder shown elsewhere in this book was a multi-year collaboration between yet another giant of knifemaking and a world-class cloisonné artist. Such collaborations extend the craft and the art, and by stimulating such work we, the collectors, make our small contributions.

Above, from the left:

Ray Appleton, USA

"Super IQ", 1993

The first "Super IQ" folder. Sculpted stainless steel blade and handle. Overall length 6 3/8" (162 mm).

"Push-Dagger", 1989

Three position folding push-dagger (from the collection of Marlene Marton), stainless steel blade, aluminum bronze handle, button lock. Overall length 5 15/16" (151 mm).

"Ray showed this knife to Marlene one day, telling her to play with it for awhile. He never got it back! In time he made her another that was just 3 1/2" (89 mm) in Overall length and it appears in David Darom's book on folders".

Opposite page, from the top:

Michael Walker, USA

"EZ slider", 1988

One of a kind lock, 6K blade, anodized titanium handle. Overall length 6 15/16" (176 mm).

"Rotating slider", 1989

One of a kind lock, 6K blade, anodized titanium and mastodon ivory handle. Overall length 6 5/8" (168 mm).

"These 2 knives have unique locking mechanisms that are the reverse of each other and that have never been made again".

"Bountiful Harvest", 1992

Unique patented blade lock folder (from the collection of Marlene Marton), stainless steel blade, anodized titanium handle engraved by Patricia Walker. Overall length 6 15/16" (176 mm).

"Metamorphosis", 1991

Unique vertical bar lock folder, stainless blade, anodized titanium handle engraved by Patricia Walker. Overall length 5 3/4" (146 mm).

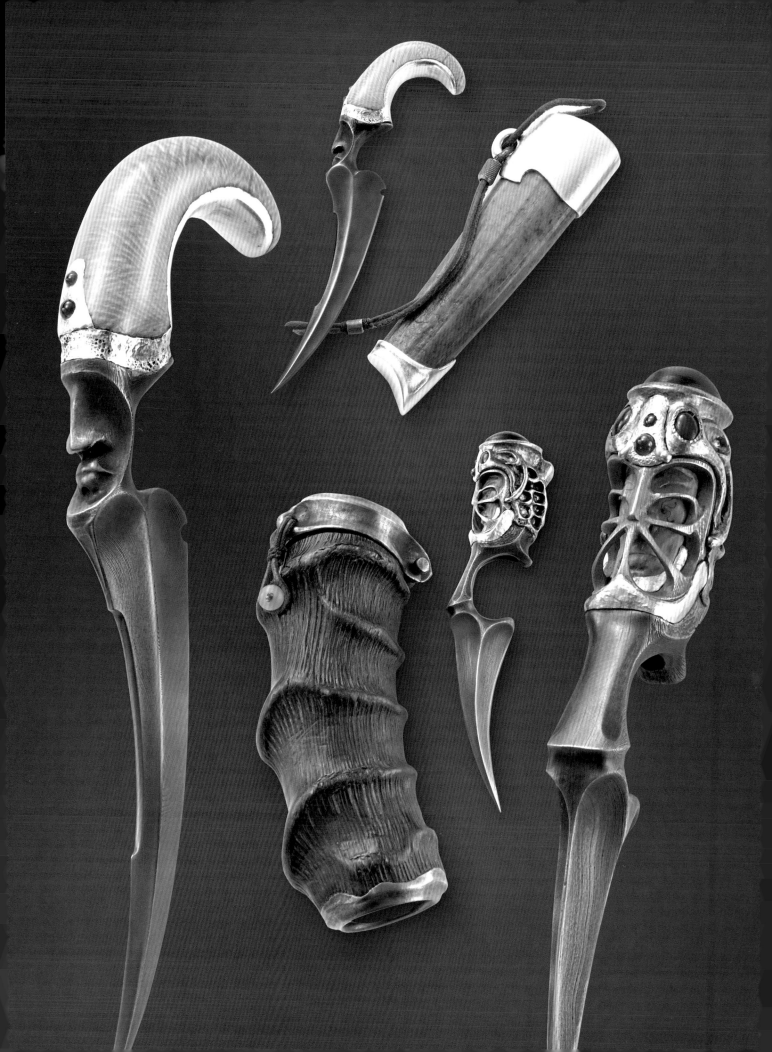

This page, from the top:
Henry Frank, USA
"Folding Dagger", 2000
Engraved and gold inlayed French
gray blade, black buffalo horn
handle, engraved gold bolsters.
Overall length 5 5/8" (143 mm).
"Gold Pen Knife", 1994
Engraved and gold inlayed French
gray blade, Mother-of-Pearl handle,
engraved gold bolsters. From the
collection of Marlene Marton,
Overall length 5 5/8" (143 mm).
*"Henry Frank's name is misspelled
on this knife, he never completed
the "R" in FRANK, so it is a "P". He
suggested that he would correct
it, but we decided that this feature
adds to the uniqueness of this
masterpiece, so it remains".*

Opposite page, from the left:
Virgil England, USA
"Shi Ak Sibu – Lord of the Wall", 2005
Pocket fighter with sheath (from the
collection of Marlene Marton), Daryl
Meier Damascus blade; mammoth
ivory, walrus ivory, emeralds, gold
and silver.
Overall length 5" (127 mm).
"Shantu Princess", 1998
Knife with case (from the collection
of Marlene Marton), Daryl Meier
Damascus blade; gold, silver, bronze,
ruby, lapis, and mammoth ivory with
scrim handle. Impala horn, case with
bronze and sterling silver.
Overall length 4 9/16" (114 mm).
*"It took years to get Virgil to craft
these pieces for Marlene, as he
wanted to make small knives that
were not just a copies of larger ones,
but ones that were free standing
creations of their own. The results
were well worth the wait".*

Left, from the top:
Matthew Lerch, USA
"West Town", 2001
Triple action liner lock with rocker bar
safety latch. Devin Thomas Damascus
blade, Robert Eggerling Damascus
and Gold-lip pearl integral handle.
Overall length 6 1/4" (159 mm).
James Schmidt, USA, *1987*
Window frame folding hunter
with lanyard lock, Damascus blade,
Damascus and antique shell handle.
Overall length 8 3/4" (222 mm).
James Schmidt, *1996*
Triple bolster lanyard lock folder,
Damascus blade, Damascus and
Black-lip pearl handle.
Overall length 7 3/8" (187 mm).

Opposite page, from the left:
Dellana, USA
"Pacific", 2005
Lock-back folder, Damascus blade,
Damascus, gold, silver, and Black-lip
pearl handle.
Overall length 6" (152 mm).
"Fire in the Sky", 1998
Lock-back folder, Damascus blade;
Damascus, gold, silver, and Black-lip
pearl handle.
Overall length 6" (152 mm).
"Although made 7 years apart, the
natural pairing of these knives is
self evident. The unique skills that
Dellana brings to knifemaking
stimulate others to advance their
own art".

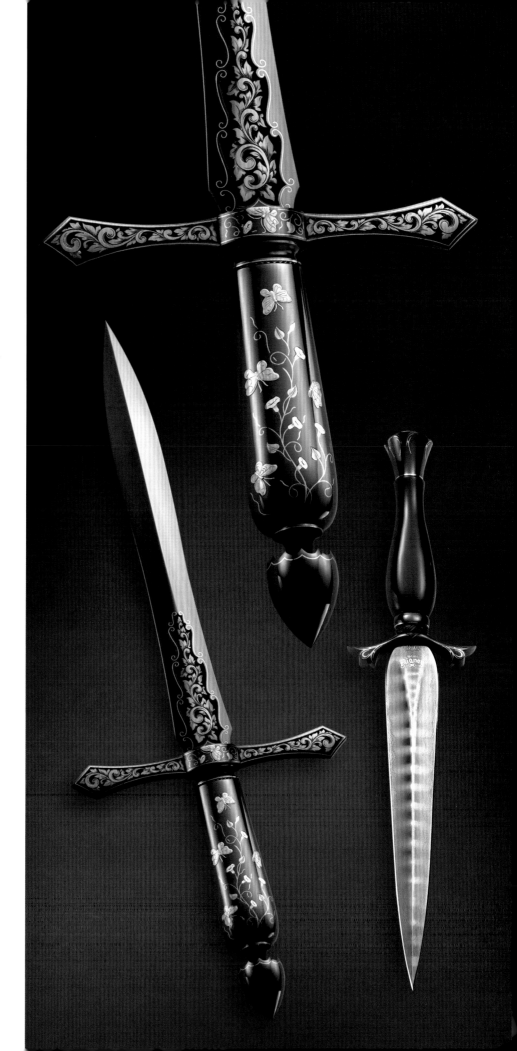

This page, from the left:

Dr. Fred Carter, USA, *1987*

First all steel dagger, blued 01 tool steel blade, blued mild steel fittings, engraved and inlayed with gold and silver.
Overall length 16 1/8" (410 mm).

"Fred provided me with my initial in depth knife education, has become a true and valued friend and is a significant motivator of my continued collecting. This particular knife is the very first all steel dagger he ever made, and he only embarked on the venture after several years of convincing. It took about 6 months to craft, as it necessitated learning and inventing new techniques to turn it into a reality".

Willie Rigney, USA, *1995*

AKI spear point dagger, Damascus blade, black jade handle, blued fittings and gold inlays by Julie Warenski.
Overall length 13" (330 mm).

Opposite page, from the left:

Buster Warenski, USA

"Dagger", 1987

440C blade with sculpted ricasso, jet (stone) handle, sculpted blued steel guard and pommel, gold inlays.
Overall length 17 1/2" (444 mm).

"Mid-Evil Dagger", 1985

Damascus blade, African blackwood handle, blued steel guard and pommel, gold inlays.
Overall length 18 5/8" (473 mm).

"This is the first knife that I obtained from Buster. It began a lifelong relationship with perhaps the man that was the most versatile of all knifemakers".

"Jambiya", 1991

Sculpted and textured 440C blade (gold inlays by Julie Warenski), white carved jade handle with gold and rubies by maker.
Overall length 15 3/16" (386 mm).

"One of Buster's favorite pieces, it was created as a result of our long term interactions, including the study of many antique Jambiyas. He surpassed the ancient masters".

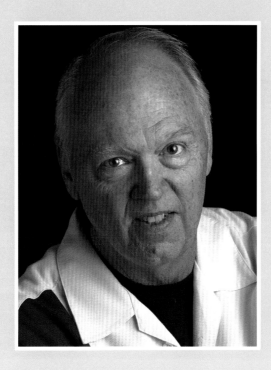

Dave Nittinger *USA*

Opposite page, from the top:
Bob Loveless, USA
"Big Bear", 2006
Desert ironwood handle.
Overall length 14" (336 mm).
"Jr Bear", 2006
Premium stag handle.
Overall length 11" (279 mm).
Joe Cordova, USA
"Marble Canoe style", 2005
Ivory and stag.
Overall length 8" (203 mm).
"Joe Cordova studied under Bob Loveless for about 5 months when Bob first came to Riverside. They are great friends today and have a true admiration for each other. Bob felt that Joe, and only Joe, could produce the hand made Canoe knife and do it correctly. I assume that Bob Loveless has asked very few makers to make a knife for his personal collection. This is one example of such a knife."

I have been collecting custom art knives since 1984. It has become a passion both for the value that anything sculptured or hand made brings to the individual but equally for the wonderful relationships that are created over the years with the great artists who made them. As time goes by I need to constrain my collection and it is for this reason that I have created my own Web Site, *www.nittingerknives.com*, and am always looking to involve others with this passion and these relationships that have become a way of life. My work career started in 1970 for Transamerica Financial and I retired after 22 years to become self-employed as a mortgage broker. My career here, helping clients refinance or purchase home loans, has given me the time to enjoy my world of custom art knives. I am always available to discuss knives and collecting them, or just deal with any questions regarding this great world of art. I hope you enjoy the pages ahead and the artistic skill it took to create the objects displayed in them. These pages are dedicated to the makers that made it all happen.

"Here is the story of the Silver Goblet, the "Maidens Mementos Loving Cup". Back in Medieval times when a young lady wished to give her man a special gift she would have a casting made of her left breast, being the closest to the heart. From this casting a beautiful goblet would be created, in silver or gold, engraved, polished and encased in a rich velvet. Hence, whenever the man would partake of his wine, his hand would be holding a pleasant personal memory. Don Hume researched this topic over 40 years ago at the UCLA library and then at the at Disney Studio's massive library. These goblets did indeed exist and now they exist again. Don Hume lives in Albuquerque, New Mexico and has been making knives for 22 years".

Above:
Don Hume, USA
"Dragon Fire", 2005
Oriental dagger with Jim Fergueson twisted nickel with 150 layers forged welded. Handle is goncalvo alves from Brazil. Six dragon heads cast in white bronze using the lost-wax casting method.
Overall length 16" (406 mm).

Opposite page, from the left:
C. Gray Taylor, USA
"Will & Fink" Style Dagger, 2003
Abalone and Mother-of-Pearl.
Overall length 10 1/2" (267 mm).
Jim Ence, USA
"Bradford", 1999
A replica of the knife made in the 1850's by Michael Price for the chief of police in San Francisco, California. The 6 1/4" (158 mm) blade is made of 440C stainless steel. Wrapped handle with dark gold walrus ivory, 24k gold buttons and shield, engraved top to bottom and around the bolster. Solid nickel-silver sheath with large oval of gold quartz and engraving.
Overall length 11" (280 mm).

Left:
Steve Likarich, USA, *2000*
With Mother-of-Pearl handle.
Overall length 11 3/4" (298 mm).
Steve Likarich, USA, *2003*
With mammoth bark ivory handle.
Overall length 12 1/4" (311 mm).
Both knives display beautiful
filework and brilliant colors of
selectively anodized titanium.

Opposite page, from the left:
Jim Sornberger, USA, *1997*
Dagger with amber, lapis, ivory and
sugalite handle.
Overall length 11 3/4" (298 mm).
Stan Fujisaka, Hawaii, *2002*
Dagger with copal, amber and
titanium handle.
Engraved by Bruce Shaw.
Overall length 13" (330 mm).
Gary Blanchard, USA, *1991*
Dagger with bloodwood handle. All
carving and engraving done by maker.
Overall length 9" (229 mm).

Left, from the top:
Dennis Friedly, USA
"Dagger", 2005
With fossil walrus handle and
Gil Ruddolph engraving.
Overall length 15" (381mm).
"Two Knives", 1999
Two Elmer Keith style knives with
elephant and lion scrimshaw by
Connie Billet.
Overall lengths 11 1/4" (286 mm).

Opposite page, from the left:
Jim Ence, USA
"Small Raccoon", 2002
440C steel blade, stag handle, 24k gold
carved raccoon, front and back.
Overall length 7" (178 mm).
"The Elephant", 2003
440C steel blade, pearl handle, 24k
gold carved elephant.
Overall length 7" (178 mm).
"Persian Dagger", 2003
The 6" (152 mm) 440C steel blade has
gold inlay on top. The nickel-silver
bolster is carved and set with 32
emeralds. Stylized handle is high quality
green jade. Matching steel sheath.
Overall length 11 1/2" (292 mm).

Above, from the left:
Stan Fujisaka, Hawaii
"Birds and Bee's", 1996
Mother-of-Pearl handle engraved by
Judy Beaver.
Overall length 6 1/2" (165 mm).
"Geisha", 2006
With dyed giraffe bone handle
engraved by Judy Beaver.
Overall length 7" (178 mm).

Opposite page, from top:
Don Maxwell, USA, *2003*
Mastodon ivory handle.
Overall length 8 1/2" (216 mm).
Larry Fuegen, USA, *2003*
Carved Mother-of-Pearl.
Overall length 8 1/4" (210 mm).
Larry Fuegen, USA, *1999*
Handle is part of an old wagon wheel.
Overall length 7 1/2" (190 mm).
Phil Boguszewski, USA, *1994*
Ivory handle.
Overall length 8 1/2" (216 mm).

Phil Boguszewski, USA, *1992*
Blue anodized titanium.
Overall length 7 3/8" (187 mm).
Koji Hara, Japan, *2005*
Mother-of-Pearl handle.
Overall length 7 1/2" (190 mm).
Dr. Fred Carter, USA, *2003*
All steel with gold dragonflies.
Overall length 7 3/4" (197 mm).
Harold Moeller, USA, *2006*
With Mosaic beetle and black water
buffalo handle.
Overall length 7 3/4" (197 mm).

Luigi Peppini *Italy*

Opposite page, from the left:
Bob Loveless, USA
"Combat", 1956
This knife is a milestone. Stacked leather-washer handle. "DELAWARE MAID" is engraved on the inferior part of the blade while the ricasso is marked "R. W. LOVELESS, MAKER, CLAYMONT, DEL." Aluminum butt. Overall length 10 9/16" (269 mm).
"Old Bowie Sub-hilt", 1955
One of the first fighters marked "R. W. LOVELESS MAKER CLAYMONT, DEL." on the blade and "139-B". The rear side, on the ricasso is "28 R.W.L." A 3 3/4" brass strip is fixed on the blade's spine. Sub-hilt and guard are brass. Stacked leather-washer handle. Aluminum butt. Overall length 12 1/2" (317 mm).
"Sub-hilt Bowie", 1968
A wonderful combat knife with the rare "Loveless and Parke" mark on the blade. Sub-hilt and guard in brass, stacked leather-washer handle with finger grooves. Aluminum butt. The rear of the blade is marked "ABERCROMBIE- FITCH. CO." Overall length 11" (279 mm).

I have always loved beautiful things but, most of all, I feel very moved meeting people who have devoted their lives to conceiving, imagining, projecting and finally manufacturing these objects - a creative process that astonishes and fascinates me. But why knives? My professional life brought me early into contact with the world of knives. With fire, forged iron, accuracy in details, the beauty of precious materials, and particularly with the "hand" of craftsmen with pride in their executions and their constant desire to create something new, to get past what has already been done, already been seen. At the beginning, the simple pleasure of possession prevailed. In this way the core of my collection was conceived. But from the beginning I also wanted to meet personally the "master knife makers", makers of the items I had picked out as the best. The more I knew them, the more I got used to their temperament and their personality, and the more I understood their creative choices. On the other hand they showed a hearty openness to accept some of my ideas and concepts. At this time a further qualitative leap occurred; it consisted in sharing the creative process with the maker. The knives I love most and am most proud of are those created from a deep exchange of ideas with the maker. A combination of experiences, tastes and different ideas that when combined together, create an original synthesis. That is why I feel such deep emotion in touching and gazing at some of my best knives: I can't forget the dialogs, the meetings, the researches - in one word, the depth of human experiences behind each of them. And so, how can I answer in a reasonable way those who ask me what are my favorite knives? Each of them has its own characteristics and, most important of all, its history made up of human relationships that make it unique and fascinating.

This page, from the left:
Bob Loveless, USA
"35 Years of Knifemaking", 1989
Commemorative hunter, stacked leather-washer handle with finger grooves. Aluminum butt. This knife is number 17 of 35 made by Loveless. Overall length 9" (228 mm).

"40 Years of Knifemaking", 1994
One knife (Lamb design), from the collector's set of 40 commemorative knives displaying all the different models made by Loveless during his first 40 years (1954-1994) of knifemaking. Green micarta handle. Overall length 8 3/16" (280 mm).

"50 Years of Knifemaking", 2005
One-of-a-kind commemorative utility knife. Desert ironwood handle. Brass/steel pins. This knife was made specially for the cover of Luigi Peppini's book, R.W. Loveless THE BOOK (2005). The most important book ever published about Bob Loveless and his 50 years of knifemaking and teaching.
Overall length 8 3/16" (280 mm).

Opposite page, from the left:
Bob Loveless, USA, *2004*
Highlights from a unique 46 knife set with amber stag handles, brass/steel pins and "R.W.L." engraved on the ricasso. The knives displayed are: Utility (11 3/8", 288 mm); Utility (9 7/8", 251 mm); Utility (8 13/16", 220 mm); Nessmuk Skinner (8 13/16", 220 mm); Gut Hook (8 13/16", 220 mm); Drop Point (8 13/16", 220 mm) and Semi-Skinner (7 9/16", 192 mm).

Opposite page, from the left:
Dietmar Kressler, Germany
Three one-of-a-kind knives with mosaic handle inlays by Jurgen Steinau (Germany), made of various pearl slices. All three blades have Kressler's old logo on the front and a new one on the rear. *"Fighter"* (8 13/16", 223 mm); *"Chute"* (8 15/16", 226 mm) and *"Dagger"* (9", 228 mm).

Above, from the right:
Collaboration Knives
Bob Loveless – Steve R. Johnson *1994*
Utility knife with amber stag handle. Marked "001" on both sides of the blade this is one of a special set of three knives.
Overall length 9 3/8" (238 mm).
Bob Loveless – Steve R. Johnson *1970*
Old utility knife with rosewood handle. A collaboration knife marked "001".
Overall length 8 5/8" (218 mm).
Bob Loveless – Barry Wood (USA) *1974*
A most unusual series of knives created by Bob and SRJ, with a machine made structure. They created the blades and Barry did the assembly. Stag and titanium handle. Named "Mark 4", this knife is marked 4-105, the fifth of 35 knives. Overall length 7 13/16" (198 mm).
Bob Loveless – Dietmar Kressler (Germany), *1976*
Stiff-horn. Sambar deer antler handle. Marled "001"
Overall length 7 1/8" (180 mm).

This page, from the top:

Bob Loveless, USA

"Drop Point Integral", 1973

Integral knife number 10. One of the most beautiful knives made by Bob Loveless. A special design made for the Safari Club in the early '80s. Ivory inlay and stag handle.
Overall length 8 3/16" (208 mm).

"Prototype Bowie", 1957

Prototype fighter style made in 8-20-57, in Claymont with a double brass guard in brass. Stacked leather-washer handle, decorated with yellow paint. The aluminum butt is shaped like a bird's head.
Overall length 11" (279 mm.)

"Hunter Prototype", 1976

Unique prototype, drop point with wide blade from the Riverside period, made the same year the "naked lady" was inaugurated. This knife has never been finished. It has never been sharpened and the end part of the pins has not been polished. Premium stag handle.
Overall length 9 7/16" (239 mm.)

Opposite page, from the left:
Ricardo Velarde, USA, 2005
Two prototypes, marked "PROTOTYPE" on the reverse side of the blade, and a one-of-a-kind knife, all with amber stag handles and hidden butts.
"Double Guard Dagger" (11 3/16", 284 mm); ***"Double guard Fighter"*** (11 5/16", 287 mm) and ***"Dagger"*** marked "001", (9 3/16", 234 mm).

This page, from the top:
Ron Lake, USA
"Gold Orion", 2000
Boot blade with lugs and a gold toothpick. Gold interframe carved by Julie Warenski in a basket weave pattern. Mirror logos and "1 of 1" marked on the blade.
Overall length 7 5/16" (185 mm).
"Pearl Orion", 2000
Boot blade with lugs and a gold toothpick. Mother-of-Pearl interframe. Mirror logos and "1 of 1" marked on the blade.
Overall length 7 5/16" (185 mm).
"Tortoise Shell Orion", 2000
Boot blade with lugs. Tortoise shell interframe with gold pins. Mirror logos and "1 of 1" marked on the blade.
Overall length 7 5/16" (185 mm).

Opposite page, from the left:
Ron Lake, USA
"Orion", 1995
All steel handle sculpted by Wolfgang Loerchner (Canada). Boot blade with mirror logos.
Overall length 7 5/16" (185 mm).
"Sierra", 2001
Steel handle with Mother-of-Pearl and Damascus inserts, sculpted by Wolfgang Loerchner (Canada). Utility blade with mirror logos.
Overall length 8 3/16" (208 mm).
"Orion", 2001
Steel handle with Damascus inserts, sculpted by Wolfgang Loerchner (Canada). Boot blade with lugs and mirror logos.
Overall length 8 3/16" (208 mm).

This page, from the left:
Francesco Pachì, Italy
"Utility Hunter", 2006
The last knife Francesco made before
retiring from custom knifemaking
and returning to professional
photography. Blued Damascus
bolster, surface elephant ivory handle
with gold pins. Marked on the spine
"F. Pachì 2006" and "My last knife".
Overall length 9 1/2" (241 mm).
"Persian Hunter", 2006
Last but one knife by Francesco, with
blued Damascus bolster, mammoth
ivory handle and gold pins. Marked
on the spine "F. Pachì 2006" and "-1".
Overall length 9 19/32" (244 mm).

Opposite page:
Michael Walker, USA
"Earth, Water, Fire, Air", 1992
Four one-of-a-kind folders, each
with a different locking mechanism.
Titanium handles, color engraved
by Patricia Walker with scenes
representing the four "elements",
earth, water, fire and air.
Overall lengths 7 1/8"-7 11/16"
(180 mm-195 mm).

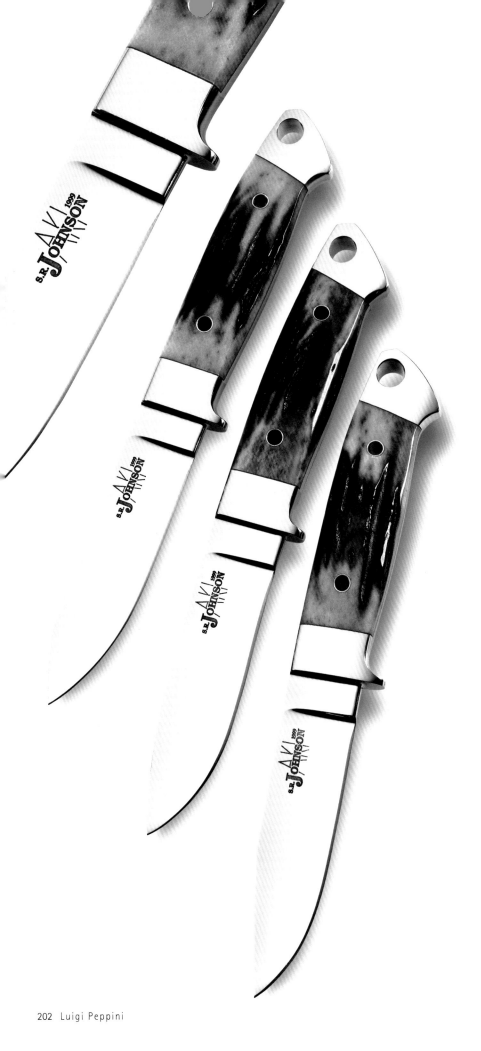

This page, from the top:
Steve R. Johnson, USA
"Three AKI Knives", 1999
"Semi-Skinner", "Skinner" and
a "Drop Point" Full Integral, all with
matching premium amber stag
handles and the special 1999 AKI
Show logo on the blade.
Overall lengths 8 3/4"-9"
(223 mm-226 mm).

Opposite page from the top:
Steve R. Johnson and Ron Lake, USA
"Sub-Hilt Fighter", 1995
Collaboration between two great
knifemakers, Steve Johnson made
the blade and Ron Lake designed
and made the handle, producing
this sub-hilt fighter. Elephant ivory
handle with gold pins.
Overall lengths 15 5/16" (389 mm).
Steve R. Johnson, USA
"Sub Hilt Fighter Giant Bear", 1995
Mammoth ivory handle, both sides
of the blade marked "001" with the
maker's logo. Overall length 16 1/4"
(412 mm). This is one of the longest
knives made by Steve Johnson.
"Sub-Hilt Bowie", 1999
Fossil walrus ivory handle. Amazing
engraving of African big game
animals by Firmo Fracassi (Italy) on
the reverse side of the blade.
Overall length 15 5/16" (389 mm).

This page, from the left:

Jack Busfield, USA, *1992*
Steel handle with Jade inlay,
engraving and gold inlay by Sam
Alfano depicting the landing
of Christopher Columbus in 1492,
made for the occasion of the
500th anniversary of the discovery
of America.
Overall length 6" (152 mm).

Steve Hoel, USA, *1991*
Steel interframe with fossil ivory
inlays. Fully engraved and gold inlaid.
Overall length 6 5/16" (160 mm).

Fred Carter, USA, *1993*
All steel engraved and gold inlaid
folding knife. 24k gold scroll work
inlaid into the handle flush with
the surface, masked, and then the
background was lightly bead blasted
to give it a frosted finish.
Overall length 5 7/8" (150 mm).

Henry H. Frank, USA, *1992*
Engraved gold bolsters, engraved
gold toothpick, engraved and gold
inlaid blade, elephant ivory handle.
Overall length 6 3/16" (157 mm).

Opposite page, from the top:
Buster Warenski, USA
"Drop Point", 1991
Jade handle, engraved and gold
inlaid by Julie Warenski.
Overall length 7 13/16" (198 mm).
"Drop Point", 1992
Elephant ivory handle, engraved by
Linton McKenzie.
Overall length 7 13/16" (198 mm).
"Skinner", 1992
Elephant ivory handle, engraved by
Julie Warenski.
Overall length 7 13/16" (198 mm).

HISTORY OF MY MARKS

This page, from the left:
Bob Loveless, USA
"Drop Point", 2003
One knife from a special set of 23 knives displaying all of the Loveless markings. Green micarta handle, brass/steel pins and "HISTORY OF MY MARKS" on the blade's spine. This is the last knife of the set with the special logo designed by Mirella Pachi and approved by Bob Loveless. Overall length 8" (230 mm).
"Wilderness Sub-Hilt", 1995
The first knife made by Loveless in 2001. Marked as such on the green canvas micarta handle, steel rivets, "RWL" on the ricasso. Engraving by Firmo Fracassi.
Overall length 12 3/8" (315 mm).
"Wilderness Sub-Hilt", 1995
Burgundy micarta handle. Logo on both sides of the blade and "ONE OF A KIND" marked on the ricasso.
Overall length 10 11/16" (272 mm).

Opposite page, from the left:
Reinhard Tschager, Italy
"Dagger", 2004
Mosaic Damascus dagger. Steel guard with Mosaic Damascus and Black-lip pearl inlays. Carved elephant ivory handle with gold pins.
Overall length 13" (330 mm).
James Schmidt, USA
"Ivory Dagger", 1973
Damascus dagger with carved elephant ivory handle.
Overall length 15 11/16" (400 mm).

Zimbabwe, Lake Kariba, June 2006

Dr. Pierluigi Peroni Italy

Opposite page:
Mirella and Francesco Pachì, Italy
"African Big Five", 2004
A one-of-a-kind collaboration between the collector and two artists, husband and wife. It is also the only existing blade with the names of both knifemaker (Francesco) and scrimshander (Mirella) in the logo. Five white mammoth ivory inserts each with a detailed scrimshaw of one of the "African Big Five" game animals. Overall length 10 7/16" (265 mm).

I have been collecting and using knives since I was a boy, and I am sure that my lifelong love for blades grew with my great passion for hunting big game in Africa. The big step towards collecting custom knives was made at the age of eighteen, when I traveled to the US for the first time. There, thanks to the legendary Mr. Nate Postner of the San Francisco Gun Exchange, I had my first chance to admire the custom blades of some well-known American knifemakers. It was truly a case of "love at first sight". Today, more than thirty years later, this passion and this love continues to shape my life. My collection is relatively small in terms of quantity, because I have always been very selective about quality. I prefer knives that are special and unique. I am rarely interested in standard or off-the-shelf pieces. Instead, I prefer to order a knife from the maker himself after developing an interesting project together with him. This way, the knife is designed and executed with input based on my experience, imagination and personal taste and the end result is of great satisfaction for me because of my contribution to its creation. In this book, I felt that I had to display some of my "special" blades, of which I am very fond. I am therefore presenting here many newly made knives never before seen in print, but also some pieces already published to which I am personally very attached.

On the left:

Ron Lake, USA

"Cimmaron" Prototypes, 2003

Two pre-patented prototype piston activated button-locking folders that led to the commercial run of Ron Lake's new design of folders produced by CRKT. These prototypes were completely hand made by Ron and have two different opening mechanisms.

Overall length 6 11/16" (169 mm).

Opposite page, from the top:

Ron Lake, USA

"Folding Boot Knife", 1997

Boot interframe folder #50 with big horn inlays. One of the first generation of Lake's Boot folders with lugs on the blade.

Overall length 7 1/4" (184 mm).

"Sierra Semi-Boot Knives", 1994

A matching set of two rare interframe folders, both blades marked #1. Big horn inlays.

Overall lengths 7 17/32" (191 mm) and 5 3/4" (145 mm).

This page, from the top:
Steve R. Johnson, USA
A set of two strange looking Lamb knives, **"Gut-Hook Lamb"** and **"Caper Lamb"**, made in 2004. Green micarta handles and different trademarks on both sides of each blade. One of the logos is the maker's signature.
Overall lengths 7 15/16" (199 mm).

Opposite page, from the left:
Steve R. Johnson, USA
"Gold Lambs", 1994
A matching set of two Lamb knives with semi-skinner and utility blades, both with serial numbers "001". Guards and fittings are 18k gold, handles are matching mammoth ivory from the same tusk.
Overall lengths 7 1/2" (196 mm).
"Pier's Hunting Knife", 1997
The blade was designed in collaboration with the collector. Stainless steel guard and premium snakewood handle. The blade is marked with the maker's logo and "ONE OF A KIND KNIFE" and with "PIER'S HUNTING KNIFE" on the reverse side.
Overall length 8 1/2" (216 mm).

S.R. JOHNSON
1966 - 2006
MANTI, UTAH

1966-2006, 40TH Anniversary
S.R. Johnson

S.R. JOHNSON
30 YEARS OF KNIVES
1966-1996

Steve Johnson

"ONE OF A KIND KNIFE"

This page, from the left:

Steve R. Johnson, USA

Two one-of-a-kind hidden tang knives with stainless steel guards and butt caps. Both made after old drawings of designs by other makers.

"Jack's Boot Knife", 1996

Made after a drawing by Jason Jacks with premium polished stag handle. Overall length 9 1/2" (240 mm).

"Loveless Delaware Skinner", 1996

Made with a fabulous snakewood handle after one of Bob Loveless' old drawings.

Overall length 8 11/16" (224 mm).

Opposite page, from the left:

Steve R. Johnson, USA

"40th Anniversary", 2006

This walrus ivory handle, one-of-a-kind knife, was made to celebrate Steve's 40 years of knifemaking, 1966-2006.

Overall length 12 3/16" (310 mm).

"30 Years of Knives", 1996

This stag handle, one-of-a-kind knife, was made to celebrate Steve's 30 years of knifemaking, 1966-1996. Overall length 13 3/4" (340 mm).

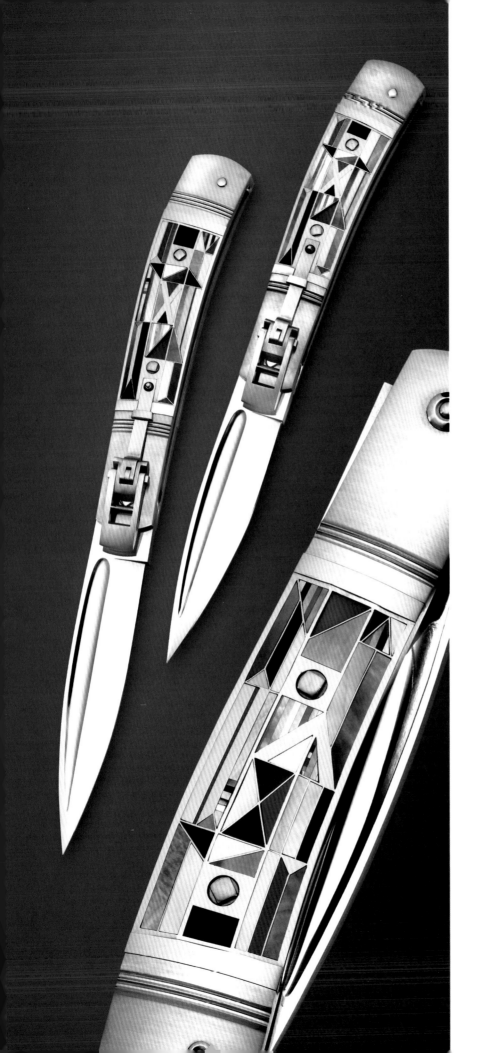

On the left;
Jurgen Steinau, Germany
"Art Deco Folders", 2001
According to Jurgen, this is his very
first matching set of folders.
The knives can be opened manually
or as an automatic. Blade is 440B
steel. Handle is made of nicorros,
a copper-nickel alloy, and is inlaid
with various pearl, stone, bakelite
and glass.
Overall lengths 8 11/16" (220 mm)
and 7 5/8" (194 mm).

Opposite page, from the left:
Jim Schmidt, USA
"Rainbow", 1995
Bolstered folding dagger with
premium Mother-of-Pearl handle.
14k gold liners and fittings and 14k
gold toothpick and tweezers.
Overall length 9 1/4" (235 mm).
"Touch of Midas", 1994
Interframe folding dagger with
fabulous Black-lip pearl inserts. 14k
gold liners and bail.
Overall length 10 1/4" (260 mm).

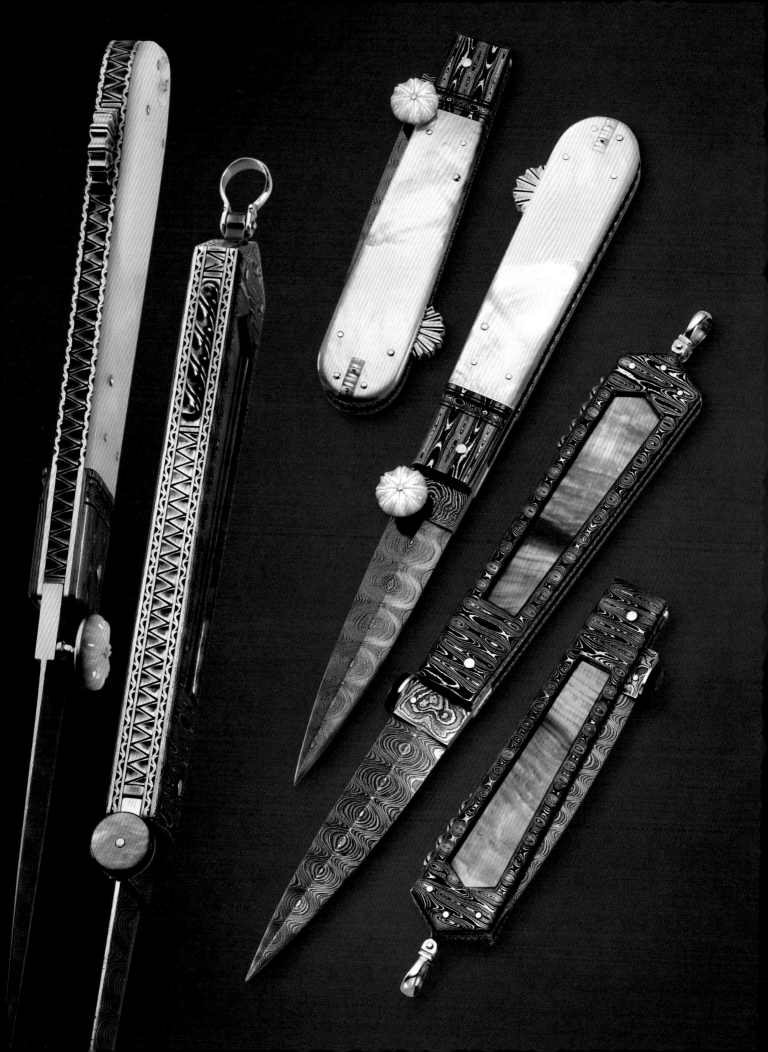

This page, from the left:

Bob Loveless, USA

Two knives that are part of a 20 piece set made in 1973 by Loveless (with the help of Steve Johnson) in his Lawndale workshop. Both have quality stag handles.

"Semi-skinner"

Overall length 8 1/2" (215 mm).

"Drop Point"

Overall length 8 5/16" (210 mm).

Opposite page, from the left:

Bob Loveless, USA

Four true one-of-a-kind knives

"R.R.R. Knife", 1976

A rare hidden tang handle, made with two separate matching slabs of premium stag.

Overall length 8 7/16" (214 mm).

"All Stainless Doctor's Knife", 1969

Specially made for a Chinese surgeon living in Los Angeles.

Overall length 8 1/8" (206 mm).

"BAD BOB'S Knife", 1970

This was "the" Bob Loveless personal knife during his Lawndale years. Hidden tang construction and crown stag handle.

Overall length 8 1/16" (204 mm).

"Proto Skinner", 1970

A very rare Loveless prototype with a walnut wood handle and open thong slot.

Overall length 7 3/8" (187 mm).

This page, from the left:
Bob Loveless, USA
"Half-Tang Knives", mid 80's
Two of about only 20 very rare half-tang knives made by Loveless. One with a smooth green micarta handle and the other with a red micarta handle and finger grooves.
Overall lengths 8 1/8" (206 mm).

Opposite page:
Reinhard Tschager, Italy
First Folding Knife, 2006
The very first folding knife made by this Italian knifemaker. A true gold knife. Frame, blade, pins and locking mechanism all made of hardened gold. Engraved by the maker and by Valerio Peli (Italy) with the collector's monogram "PLP" set in diamonds.
Overall length 4 7/16" (112 mm).

This page, from the left:
Richard Hehn, Germany
"Integral Folder", 2002
Handle inserts are mammoth ivory.
Overall length 7 1/32" (178 mm).
"Fixed-Blade", 2002
Integral construction with
alternating inserts of light and dark
pieces of desert ironwood.
Overall length 7 9/16" (192 mm).

Opposite page, from the left:
Six true "Pocket Knives"
Ron Lake, USA, *1996*
Watch-pocket folder number #1, this is Ron Lake's smallest interframe.
Stainless steel frame and Mother-of-Pearl inlays.
Overall length 4 9/16" (116 mm).
Richard Hodgson, USA, *1994*
The smallest interframe folder made by the late Richard Hodgson.
Premium Black-lip pearl inlays. Overall length 5 3/32" (129 mm).
Jurgen Steinau, Germany, *2004/2005*
Small scale auto/manual folder with assorted-pearl mosaic handle.
Overall length 4 3/4" (120 mm).
Steve Hoel, USA, *1992*
Pocket-folder interframe with tiger eye inlays.
Overall length 5 1/2" (140 mm).
Salvatore Puddu, Italy, *2006*
Watch-pocket folder with ancient tortoise shell inlays and a gold bail.
Overall length 4 21/32" (118 mm).
Charlie Bennica, France, *2005*
Pocket folder with premium Black-lip pearl inlays in the handle. Two
inserts on the right side and a single, larger one, on the reverse side.
Overall length 5 3/32" (129 mm).

On the left:
Francesco Pachì, Italy
"Little Tanto", 2000
Carbon steel Damascus blade,
premium and matching tiger coral
handle slabs, 18k gold pins.
Overall length 6 11/16" (169 mm).

Opposite page, from the left:
Emmanuel Esposito, Italy
"Snakewood Integrals", 2006
Two Semi-Integrals and one Full-
Integral with unique designs and
exotic snakewood handles are the
work of this young and extremely
talented Italian knifemaker.
Overall lengths 8 3/16" (207 mm),
7 13/16" (199 mm) and 7 1/16"
(178 mm).

Opposite page from the left:
Ray Appleton, USA

"I was lucky to have met Ray during his first visit to the Custom Knife Show in Solvang (California), in April 1986. He opened his briefcase with 14 stunning knives. It was a breathtaking moment. Ray numbered and named most of his knives".

"Lagonda" #22, 1986
D-2 blade with triple hollow grind. Ebony and brass handle. Double Star lock that locks open in 10 different positions.
Overall length 7 1/4" (184 mm).

"Jason" #54, 1988
D-2 hardened blade and body. Infilock that locks in any position after releasing the rotating buttons on both sides.
Overall length 7 3/4" (197 mm).

"Haley's Comet" #14, 1986
Blade is 416 stainless steel, brass inlay in the handle. The first "I.Q." folder. Opens all the way but needs one's I.Q. to close the blade.
Overall length 5 3/4" (145 mm).

"Last Chance" # 17, 1986
Blade is 416 stainless steel, Ray's first with a triple hollow grind. Round double button lock with 7 locking positions.
Overall length 5 3/4" (145 mm).

"Howdy spook" #2, 1984
Ray's second knife. Blade is 416 stainless steel, copper and brass inlays in the handle. Star multilock.
Overall length 5 1/8" (130 mm).

"Wilderness B", 1984
Ray's fourth knife. Blade is 416 stainless steel, Pop-up round double locking button.
Overall length 5 1/8" (130 mm).

Wolf Schulz-Tattenpach Germany

Born in Berlin, in 1938, Wolf grew up in Braunschweig, Germany, the son of a well-known sculptor and painter. He planned to become an industrial designer and began going to art school at night and working as a journeyman automobile mechanic during the day. His military service was spent as an aircraft mechanic, and later he became a master miller and engineer for flour-milling machinery. In 1965, Wolf followed his girlfriend, Brigitte, to Sydney. They married and he worked as an engineer for about a year. A two week vacation in San Francisco ended up with them staying there for 25 years - Brigitte with three boutiques and Wolf with a repair shop for Volkswagen and Porsche on the Golden Gate Park. In the early 1980s, Wolf and Brigitte bought a Paul W. Poehlman knife at the San Francisco Gun Exchange after meeting the owner, Nate Posner. Brigitte liked its clean design, Wolf was fascinated with the workmanship and the stability of the locking mechanism. After meeting Bernard R. Levine, knife expert and author of many books, Wolf decided to collect knives that have unusual locking mechanisms. He also got to meet Paul W. Poehlman, a design engineer and industrial artist working for an aeronautical hardware company as director of advanced designing. In 1974 Paul came up with the "Rotating Axial Lock" situated between the blade and the handle and created his first limited edition of eight unique folders. Wolf still considers Paul's knives his favored tool in the pocket. During those years, Wolf and Brigitte attended many knife shows in the USA and Europe. In 1990, they moved back to Braunschweig and opened a cutlery store, which they sold in 2004.

On the left:

Paul Fox, USA

"Electric Folding knife", 1984

In 1984, Wolf met Paul Fox at the Guild Show in Kansas City, where this knife won the prize for the Most Innovative Knife of the year. On one side the knife is engraved, "Paul Fox" with the outline of a fox head and numbered "No1 of 1". The handle is titanium and has two nail-slots. One to open the blade and the other to close it. The reverse side houses the electric motor - 8000 rpm with a 400:1 ratio gear box. The motor is activated by three #CR2032 3.0V batteries. Two to open the ATS-34 blade, one to close it. The blade is held in place and rotates between 2 ball bearings.

Overall length 8 15/16" (227 mm).

Opposite page, from the top:

Michael Walker, USA

"Prototype", 1986

Blade is 154CM, with "Walker's Lockers by Michael L. Walker" on one side and "001 PAT. PEND" on the other. The entire body of the knife is made of blue anodized titanium. The scales are ebony and fastened with self-made titanium screws. Depressing the button unlocks the blade that is opened by turning the serrated end with one's index finger. It locks open. Overall length 5 15/16" (168 mm).

"Prototype", 1985

"Early in 1985, Michael asked me if I would like to have a cup of coffee with him. So we did and he pulled out this knife and showed it to me. He had just applied for a Patent for its locking mechanism. I was allowed to show it only to my wife, until in December, his Patent was granted". Blade is 154CM, with "Walker's Lockers by Michael L. Walker" on one side and and "Prototype CM" on the other. Checkered ebony handle. Overall length 5 15/16" (150 mm).

"Experimental Liner Lock", 1983

This early experimental liner lock is the first integral style liner lock (frame lock). It was also the first knife with a tiny steel ball in the liner to prevent the blade from opening accidentally. This folder passed a lock breaking pressure test of 30 foot/pounds. The blade has a welded cutting edge and the body is made of titanium. Overall length 6" (152 mm).

Above:
Timothy Leatherman, USA
Leatherman PST, 1983

"In 1983, at a custom knife show in Eugene (Oregon), a young man by the name of Tim Leatherman, came to our table and asked Peter (my partner) and me to visit his table, but come over one at a time. I went first, and his table was cluttered with various pliers, blades, screwdrivers, files and saws - about 30 different tools. Tim asked me for my idea of a practical combination of these bits to fit into two handles. When Peter's turn came, he chose the same pieces I did. Tim then asked us if we thought that a multi-purpose tool like that would sell and we said yes. I gave him my card and ordered one there and then. On May 7th, 1983 I was holding the first Leatherman PST. 23 years later, Timothy and his wife stayed with us in Germany for a day. During the years that passed since we first met, he had sold more than 30 million Leatherman tools".
Size: 4"x1"x1/2" (112x27x12 mm).

Opposite page from the left:
Robert E. Hayes, USA

It took Bob Hayes twelve years as a knifemaker to come up with his own knife design. He lived in a trailer, deep in the forest in the foothills of the Sierra Nevada with no electricity. Surrounded only with files, saws, sandpaper and a hand drill, the accuracy of his fit and finish are amazing.

"Button Lock" #4, 1980
A spring loaded locking pin, situated in a half-moon cutout on the base of the blade, is activated by a button on the handle to unlock the 440C blade. Stainless steel body and ebony scales. Overall length 5 1/2" (140 mm).

"Button Lock" #9, 1983
Same locking mechanism as the previous knife. Blade is 440C with a flat grind on the left side only. Stainless steel body, black delrin spacer and Mother-of-Pearl scales. Overall length 6 7/8" (173 mm).

"Mid lock" #1, 1979
The 154CM blade is marked "#1", handle slabs are ivory paper micarta. Overall length 8" (200 mm).

"Bolster lock", 1977
One of Hayes' earlier knives with a guard sticking out. When closed, the guard sticks out on top. Putting pressure on the guard while pressing the bolster lock leaver, shoots the blade out like a switchblade. As this mechanism uses a "human spring" it is a legal carry knife. The 154CM blade is stamped "#1". Nickel-silver bolster and Mother-of-Pearl handle.
Overall length 7" (180 mm).

"Bolster lock", 1982
Same locking mechanism as on the previous knife. When closed, a serrated part of the blade protrudes, to enable swinging it open smoothly with ones index finger. The 440C blade is marked "#1" and is ground only on the left side. Black delrin spacer, stainless steel handle with ivory.
Overall length 6" (152 mm).

Left, from the top:

Paul William Poehlmann, Canada

"Series II Model 2", 1995

Prototype. Blade is 440C, side plates are hardened 410 stainless steel, scales are ivory micarta. Spacer has 2 hidden set screws to limit radial play. Between the years 1996 and 1997 Petersen Precision Engineering manufactured 25,000 of these knives (with black zytel scales) sold by Gerber.
Overall length 6 1/2" (165 mm).

"Prototype 2P", 1976

Paul started making three models, 3P (big), 2P (medium) and 1P (small). Gerber produced about 85,000 knives of Model 2P with various scales. Only prototypes have an articulated lanyard loop and the left side is marked "PAUL MODEL 2P". Ivory micarta scales. Overall length 6" (152 mm).

"Paul Pocket", 2001

This knife has two set-screws built into the blade to eliminate radial play. 440C blade is marked "Series 1 Model 1". Ivory micarta scales. In 2002, Jim Wehrs, owner of "Lone Wolf Knives", asked Paul to help him build the "Paul Pocket" knife. There are 6 different patented models using Paul's lock, 35,000 have already been sold. Overall length 5 1/8" (130 mm).

"Limited Edition Folder", 1978

Paul's 10th limited edition folder. 440C blade is marked "POEHLMANN" on one side and "#1" on the other. The sides of the bolsters are designed to conceal the tang when the knife is closed. Overall length 5" (127 mm).

"Prototype Model 1P", 1976

Paul's first design of the 1P for Gerber, but it was never manufactured. It is Paul's smallest Knife. 154CM blade is marked "Paul, Model 1P" on one side, "by GERBER Portland, ORE. USA". Cocobolo scales, and articulated lanyard loop.
Overall length 5" (127 mm).

Opposite page, from the top:

Paul William Poehlmann, Canada

"Limited Edition Skinner", 1979

Paul's 14th limited edition folder, #1 of 3, ivory micarta scales and an articulated lanyard loop. The 440C blade is marked "Poehlmann" and "#1". Overall length 9 1/4" (234 mm).

"Limited Edition Drop Point", 1979

Paul's 13th limited edition folder, #1 of 3, with a 440C drop point blade. Overall length 8 7/8" (226 mm).

"Limited Edition Model P33", 1976

Paul's 7th limited edition folder, #2 of 8. 154CM drop point blade is marked "Prototype, 2B" with "PAUL" on the spine. Side plates and bolsters were milled out of one piece of ARMCO17-4 stainless steel. Black ebony scales. Overall length 8 7/8" (226 mm).

"Limited Edition", 1976

Paul's 8th limited edition folder, #1 of 12. 154CM blade is marked "PAUL" and "#1". Side plates and spacer are 7075 T6 Al.Al and stamped "Paul, Prototype", "#1", "11.76" and "#1 of 12". Ivory micarta scales.
Overall length 6 3/16" (157 mm).

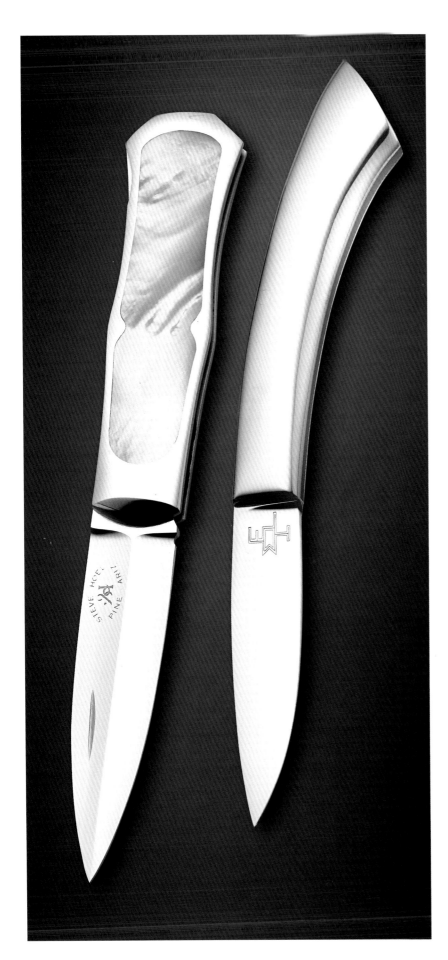

This page, from the left:

Steve Hoel, USA

"Large Coke Bottle", 1982

"Once in a while, I see something that is so pretty and so well executed that I forget my principles and buy a knife with a "standard" locking mechanism. This is what happened with Hoel's back lock folder".

The 154CM spear point blade is stamped "#01". Mother-of-Pearl interframe.

"Years later I showed Steve the knife, and he said that it was the only one he ever made with this blade design".

Overall length 7" (177 mm).

Billy Mace Imel, USA

"Slip-Joint Folder", 1979

"Here comes the ultimate "blunder". This knife doesn't even have a lock... But it was Brigitte's (a sculptor herself) favored knife design, and she could not resist buying it".

Blade and strong back spring are 440C and the side plates are 303 stainless steel. The blade has Billy's logo engraved on it and the spacer is marked "#105". When closing the knife, the blade stops midways, so that one can get the fingers out of the way. This is the largest model of the three versions. Overall length 7 3/4" (172 mm).

Opposite page, from the left:

Jurgen Steinau, Germany

Jürgen started as a well known sculptor in East Berlin and his works can be found in museums and private collections. In 1985 he began creating long foldable knife-objects with geometrical inlay work in the handle, Being isolated in East Germany, he realized that he was not the only custom knifemaker in the world only after attending his first knife show in 1988.

"Prototype", 1991

The blade is made of X90CrMoV18 steel, body, spring and lock are X40Cr13 steel. Inlays are horn and Mother-of-Pearl in a nickel frame. Overall length 8 1/4" (210 mm).

"Knife Objects", 1994

A set of two knife-objects made from X90CrMoV18 steel. The inlays are Mother-of-Pearl and bakelite. Overall length 7 3/4" (203 mm) and 2 1/4" (56 mm).

Opposite page, from the left:

Jim and Joyce Minnick, USA

*"These two unique works of art are
the products of a collaborating
husband and wife team - Jim and
Joyce Minnick. From the varying
textures in the blade steel to the
engraving themes executed by Joyce
these are truly excellent examples of
the knifemaker's art at its finest".*

"Celtic Wizard", 2000

Mild steel in both the blade and
frames with a black oxide treatment.
Various textures and carving on
blade and frames. Black-lip pearl
inlays in the frames and spine.
Figural engraving with gold inlay
and French gray technique plus
some gold raised figures adding
a third dimension to the engraving.
All engraving by Joyce. There is a
diamond in the button.
Overall length 7" (178 mm).

"King of the Seas", 2001

Blade and frames are of mild steel
with a black oxide finish. Inlays are
exhibition grade Mother-of Pearl.
Textured blade and bolsters and
carvings with dramatic juxtaposition
of glossy and matte areas giving
great drama to those areas. The
figural engraving and gold inlays
are by Joyce. The gold inlays and the
French graying technique create a
dramatic contrast. A diamond is set
into the release button and the spine
is fileworked.
Overall length 7 1/2" (190 mm).

Ron Stagnari USA

Born, raised and living all my life in New Jersey makes me the prototypical
"Jersey Guy". In 1986 I started my own business in the graphic arts finishing
industry. On the recreational side, with my wife Denise, our children and
granddaughter, we boat and fish in summer and ski in winter. I have
always been fascinated by knives never knowing how many people shared
my interest or created these works of art. Attended my first New York
Custom Knife Show and continued from there. After learning the ropes
and with my business enjoying a modest level of success, I realized that
if my collection was to be considered a good one, it should consist of
one-of-a-kind pieces or at least very limited edition knives. That was the
direction I have chosen for the last ten years, and I like to think that my
approach is more cerebral. The knives that I obtain are not inexpensive
and I enjoy taking my time examining those pieces and conversing with
the knifemakers about the materials and features of each piece. When I
have done that, I usually leave the table to quietly consider how the knife
fits in my collection and whether I feel that it is truly unique. Only after
these considerations will I decide whether to make the purchase. The two
things I enjoy most are collecting a particular maker over time, watching
the development of his craft and secondly, working in collaboration with a
maker or with a maker collaborating with another craftsman and actually
having a hand in designing a particular knife. My preferences are darkish
Damascus designs (preferably multi-bar patterns), dagger or Persian shapes
set off by exhibition grade pearl and great engraving, including some gold.
I also love Wharncliff shaped blades when they are properly ground.

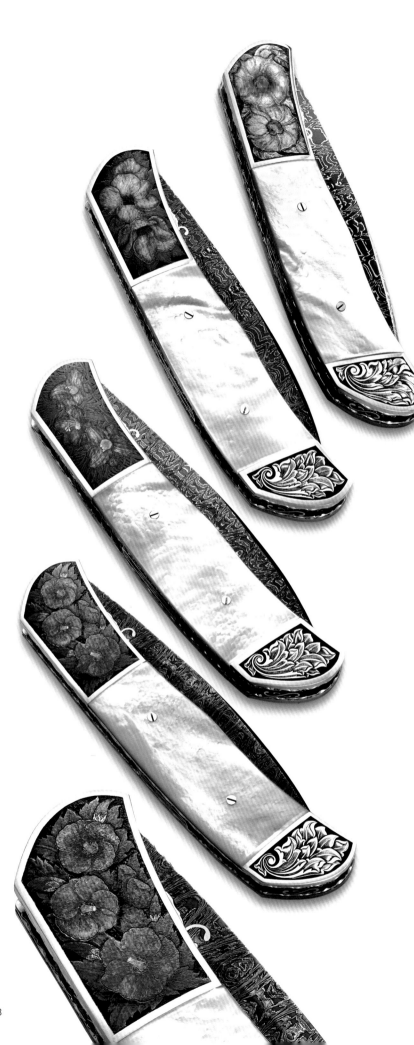

John W. Smith, USA
"Seasons", 2004 to 2006
"Shown on both facing pages is a set of knives that John W. Smith recently completed for me. We worked together to come up with the theme and decided that the four seasons depicted as women by Mucha would be a perfect choice. The front bolsters show colored engravings representing the four seasons as women, while the opposite sides of the knives display colored engravings of flowers that pick up the colors from the front sides of the knife".

A set of four automatic knives with thematic engravings. Blade material is John's Damascus mixture of 1084, 15w20 and nickel. The bolsters are 416 stainless steel heat-treated for engraving. The spine and the liners are completely fileworked. There is gold inlay with 24k gold wire in the top of the blade, in his logo on the blade, on the spine and in the engraving on the rear bolsters. Each knife is constructed with 14k gold screws and with the central pin hidden below the front bolster so the engraving is uninterrupted. Overall lengths 7 5/8" (194 mm).

This page, from the left:
Glenn Waters, Japan
"Ju Go Ya Folder", 2002
Blade is Devin Thomas Damascus with 14k gold thumb stud and a cognac diamond. Handle is 14k green gold, pink gold, white gold and silver. 2 yellow diamonds, 7 white diamonds, 1 ruby and 24k gold inlays. 15 rabbits in various precious metals decorate this knife and depict the rabbits as an old Japanese tradition for a bountiful harvest.
Overall length 5 1/2" (140 mm).

"Riyu Jin Folder", 2000
Double action liner lock folder. Blade material is ZDP-189 and ATS-34 *Sanmai* style, engraved, 24k gold inlays and an 18k gold thumb stud with ruby. Handle is *Shibu ichi jin* inlaid with 18k gold, 24k gold, silver and *Shyaku dou*, 2 lab grown rubies and mammoth bark ivory slabs. Back bar, ATS-34 fully fileworked, engraved and inlaid with 24k gold. Fully fileworked anodized titanium liners.
Overall length 10 1/2" (267 mm).

Opposite page, from the left:
Glenn Waters, Japan
"As with all of Glenn s art work there is a distinctive Asian influence. All his knives have themes and are executed with a lot of gold, silver, stones, engraving and carving".
"Fu-Ra Jin Folder", 2003
Limited edition folder #2/100. Blade is Ladder pattern Damascus with pearl inlaid thumb stud. Silver handle with ruby fireballs thrown by the wind and storm gods and 18k gold lightning inlays. An under stated approach by Glenn but still distinctively his style.
Overall length 5 1/4" (133 mm).

"Egyptian Folder", 2000
Blade is Twist pattern Damascus with 14k gold carved pyramid as a thumb stud. Silver handle with an inlaid lapis scarab and a raised 14k white gold escutcheon of an ankh. Other Egyptian carvings and a mystery transistor thrown in on each side of the knife. Carved spine with scarabs and inlaid 24k ankh, scarab and small Black-lip pearl inserts.
Overall length 4 13/16" (123 mm).

This page, from the top:

Jim and Joyce Minnick, USA

"On these two pages we can see the continuing development of Joyce's carving and her moving on to engraving and gold inlays".

"Gentleman's auto folder", late '90s

Robert Eggerling's Crossroads pattern Damascus blade and bolsters, lightly etched to give them texture. Caramel mammoth ivory handle, fluted and wound with 24k gold twisted wire. Fully fileworked titanium liners anodized to a purple shade and a fully fileworked spine.
Overall length 7 1/2" (190 mm).

"Coffin Handled Auto Dagger", 1999

Jerry Rados Ladder pattern Damascus blade. Caramel colored mammoth ivory fluted handle wound with 24k twisted gold wire. Fully fileworked titanium liners anodized to a blue shade.
Overall length 8 1/2" (216 mm).

"Gents Folder", 1995

Mild steel blade and bolsters with black oxide finish. Handle material is "Pink Ivory" African wood. Art Deco engraving and gold inlays by Joyce on the bolsters.
Overall length 6 1/2" (165 mm).

Opposite page, from the left:

Jim and Joyce Minnick, USA

"Art Deco Auto Dagger, 2002

Black oxide treated mild steel blade and bolsters. Pre-ban elephant ivory elegantly carved by Joyce. French grayed engraving on bolster with gold inlays.
Overall length 8 1/2" (216 mm).

"Ladies Back Lock Folder", 2000

Black oxide treated mild steel blade and bolsters. Pre-ban fluted elephant ivory. Carving and gold inlays by Joyce. Overall length 7" (178 mm).

"Two Dress folders", 1994 and 1995

Devin Thomas ladder pattern Damascus blades etched to bring out the pattern. Blackened mild steel bolsters with Joyce's French grayed engraving and gold inlays. Exhibition grade Mother-of-Pearl handles.
Overall lengths 8" (203 mm) and 6 1/2" (165 mm).

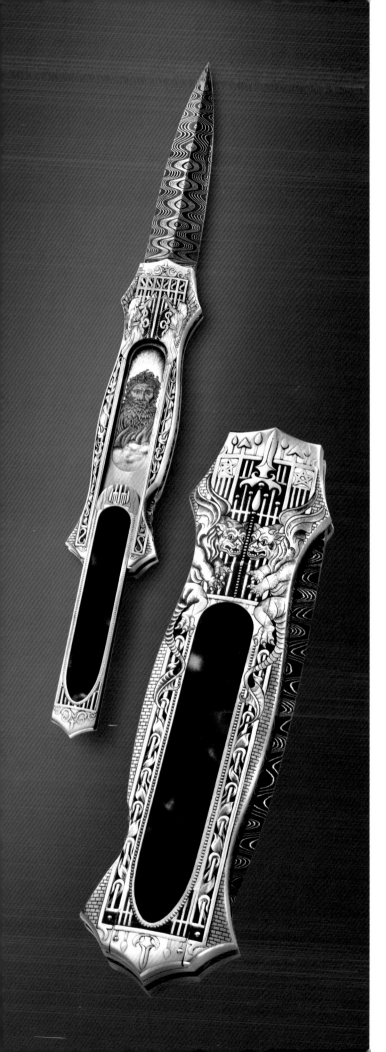

This page:
Joe Kious and Julie Warenski, USA
"The Gates of Good and Evil" 2004-2005
A double pocket locket gent's folder. Mike Norris Ladder pattern Damascus blade and a 416 stainless steel handle heat-treated for engraving. Antique tortoise shell inlays.
"Julie agreed with me on a Good versus Evil concept and she engraved a masterpiece".
Overall length 6 3/8" (162 mm).

Opposite page and below:
Loyd McConnell, USA
"Seascapes", 1991
A set of 8 knives and one prototype with sea life themes, housed in a scallop shell shaped wooden case. The blade material is Jerry Rados Ladder pattern Damascus and the handle materials consist of various types of marine coral and shell. Two knife handles are apple coral, two handles are tiger coral, two are Gold-lip pearl and two are pink pearl. The third pink pearl knife is a prototype. A different sea creature is engraved and inlaid in gold by Laura Stenhouse (Blankenship) on each bolster.
Overall lengths 7" (178 mm).

Opposite page, from the left:
C. Gray Taylor, USA
"Lobster Folder", 1997
Damascus blade and nail file,
18k gold toothpick and bale, 416
stainless steel side plates engraved
by Tim George with Victorian
continuous leaf scroll, with 24k gold
folds, deep relief background and
finely shaded leaves.
Length closed 3" (76 mm).
Dwight Towell, USA
"Interframe Folding Dagger", 1999
2 3/4" (70 mm) blade made of
154CM steel. Handle is engraved in
French gray and gold with Black-lip
pearl oval inlay bordered in gold,
engraved by maker.
Length closed 3 3/4" (95 mm).
Buster Warenski, USA
"Reverse Congress Style", 2005
Buster's only spring back folder, with
two 3" (76 mm) clip point blades.
Engraved and inlaid bolsters by Julie
Warenski marked Warenski on tang
and J. Warenski and No.1 on frame,
Mother-of-Pearl scales.
Length closed 4" (102 mm).
C. Gray Taylor, USA
"Gunstock Lobster Folder", 2001
Two 1 3/4" (44 mm) blades and a 2"
(51 mm) spear point blade and nail
file made of 440C stainless steel. 416
stainless liners, pearl scales with gold
pins and escutcheons. Engraved by
Tim George.
Length closed 3 1/4" (82 mm).

Edward Stitt *USA*

I believe my interest in knives began, at least subconsciously, the day I was
born. I was born on my brother's 6th birthday. When it turned out that I
was the birthday gift he had been promised, he was quite disappointed. He
was expecting a pocket knife. Of course it was many years before he gave
up reminding me of this, so naturally I have always felt that knives were
very important. Consequently, although only my later years have qualified
me as a collector of knives, my whole life I have been an acquirer of knives.
So, I have in my possession many knives which would have little value to
any one but me, one of which is a tiny pen knife, two inches long which I
found in the early '40s and was probably made sometime in the l920s or
1930s. It is a prized possession. My discovery of handmade knives at the
end of the 1970s led me to start collecting and also to open a small cutlery
store in Carmel, California. There I spent ten very interesting years getting
to know many gifted knife makers and collectors from the world over.
For some reason they seem to be the finest and most interesting people
I have ever come to know and I consider it a privilege to be accepted as a
member of this group. My collection has grown considerably since I sold
"Carmel Cutlery" in 1994, and no longer have people coveting the knives
I would like to keep for my own pleasure.

Opposite page, from the top:
Henry Frank, USA
"Upswept Folder", 1997
Made for the San Diego AKI Show.
Ivory handle with 14k gold pins, 14k
gold toothpick, blade engraved with
oak leaves and acorns inlaid in 24k
gold, lock lever and spring engraved
and inlaid in 24k gold, 14k gold
engraved bolsters, 14k gold liners.
All work by maker.
Overall length 5 3/4" (146 mm).

"New Bolster Design", 1996
The 2 1/4" (57 mm) blade is French
grayed and with fine scroll engraving,
repeated on 14k gold bolsters. Ivory
handle with 14k gold pins and two
14k gold ovals inlaid in ivory. French
grayed back spring engraved and
inlayed with 24k gold, 14k gold liners.
Overall length 5 1/2" (140 mm).

"Small Pen-Knife", 1997
Ivory handle with 14k gold engraved
pins, engraved bolster and liners.
Blade lined with 24k gold and
engraved with fine scroll and French
grayed finish. Two 14k gold inlays in
fired enamel inlaid in the ivory.
Overall length 5" (127 mm).

This page, from the left:
Steven Rapp, USA
"Dog-Bone Bowie", 2005
Elegant gentleman's knife, styled after
early American Bowies. Mammoth
ivory handle with silver studs and
escutcheon plates, 416 stainless steel
sheath, all engraved by Julie Warenski.
Blade length 10 1/8" (257 mm).

Larry Fuegen, USA
"California Bowie", 1999
Forged carbon steel 8 1/4" (159 mm)
blade, cream colored fossil walrus
ivory handle, deep carved with floral
design in 1850's San Francisco style.
Textured sterling silver and carved
14k gold guard calfskin covered
sheath with sterling silver and 14k
gold fittings.
Overall length 11" (279 mm).

Opposite page, from the left:

Joe Kious, USA

"Gentleman s Interframe Pocket Knife", 2005

ATS-34, Black-lip pearl scales, file worked back spring and blade. Engraving and gold inlay by Julie Warenski.
Length closed 3 1/4" (82 mm)

Tim Herman, USA

"Damascus Sliver", 1999

Elegant side lock folder, all stainless Damascus, hand filed and polished flutes from blade tip widening as it nears the butt.
Overall length 8 1/2" (mm).

Jim Sornberger, USA

"San Francisco Style Liner Lock", 2002

Nickel-silver side plates inlaid with sixteen-to-one mine (California's last gold quartz mine) gold quartz and engraved by maker.
Overall length 6 3/4" (171 mm).

Dwight Towell, USA

"Lock Back Folder", 1995

Marked 001. African blackwood handle with abalone and 24k gold inlay in scroll pattern. English scroll engraving on bolsters, file work on back of blade. All work by maker.
Overall length 8" (203 mm).

John W. Smith, USA

"Lapis Interframe Folder", 2005

Damascus blade and file worked spacer, back of blade inlaid with 24k gold. Hidden screw construction with 416 stainless frames engraved with 24k gold inlay. File worked liners and 18k gold thumb stud.
Overall length 7 1/2" (1990 mm).

Scott Slobodian, USA

"Cherry Blossom", 2005

Ku Boo liner lock folder, 3 1/4" (82 mm) blade is made of Devin Thomas' spriograph stainless Damascus. Frame is titanium with .9999 fine silver scales, .9999 fine gold is fused to silver with ancient technique called Keum Boo. Engraved by Barbara Slobodian.
Overall length 7 1/4" (184 mm).

Above, from the left:

S. R. Johnson, USA

"Dropped Point Narrow-Tang Hunter", 2001

Stag handle with mammoth ivory spacer and mokume butt cap. Blade is 3 3/4" (95 mm). Overall length 8 3/4" (222 mm).

C. K. Fortenbury, USA

"Sgian Dubh", late 1970s

Knife with a 3 3/4" (95 mm) Damascus blade by the late great Don Hastings. African blackwood handle is capped both ends with sterling silver thistle design. Shown from backside with Hastings stamped in the blade. Front of handle is carved basket-weave design, Lapis stone imbedded in butt cap. Overall length 7" (178 mm).

Ted Dowell, USA

"Intregal Hilt & Cap Hunter", 1993

D2 steel blade, mammoth ivory handle. Engraved by Julie Warenski. Overall length 9" (228 mm).

"Mini Integral Hilt & Cap Drop Point Hunter", 1997

D2 steel blade, tan old walrus ivory handle. Hilt and cap engraved by Julie Warenski. Overall length 5 3/4" (146 mm).

Opposite page, from the left:
Buster Warenski, USA
"Lady Finger", 1993
Dagger with a 6 3/4" (171 mm) 440C
blade. The black marble handle is
carved with small flowers in spiral
flutes. Guard and crown shaped butt
cap are blackened steel engraved
and trimmed in gold inlay, amethyst
stone in end of handle.
Overall length 11" (279 mm).
"Classic Dagger", 1999
9" (228 mm) 440C blade, carved
black marble handle with nickel-
silver fittings fully carved and
sculpted. Nickel-silver sheath is
engraved with fine French greyed
leaf and scroll design. All engraving
and sculpting by Julie Warenski.
Overall length 14 1/2" (368 mm).

Right:
Buster Warenski, USA
"Integral Utility Sheath-Knife", 2000
Utility knife with a 3 1/2" (89 mm)
440C blade, interframe handle inlaid
with cocobolo wood and engraved
sterling silver. Engraving repeated on
nickel-silver sheath, engraving
by Julie Warenski.
Overall length 7 1/2" (190 mm).
Jim Ence, USA
"Mini Boot Knife", 2005
Premium grade Mother-of-Pearl
handle with wide butt flair. Bolsters
and sheath engraved and set with
rubies by maker.
A 4 1/2" (114 mm) 440C blade.
Overall length 9 3/4" (248 mm).

On the left:
Jim Ence, USA
"Will and Finck" California Style Dagger, 2005
A 8 1/2" (216 mm) 440C blade. Abalone mosaic handle has leaf and scroll engraving, repeated on nickel silver handle wrap, guard and sheath. Engraved by maker.
Overall length 12" (305 mm).

Opposite page, from the top:
James Schmidt, USA
"Old King", 1992
Damascus blade, back spring, and bolsters. File worked back spring, blade and liners. Lanyard-ring lock, fossilized mastodon ivory handle.
Overall length 9" (228 mm).
"Frog Fur", 1998
Drop point folding hunter. Blade 384 layers of 203E and W2 steel. Bolsters are nickel 200 and iron with black enamel finish. Nickel-silver file worked liners. Handle is striped chocolate brown, black, and white fossilized walrus ivory. 14k gold lanyard ring.
Overall length 7" (178 mm).
"Baby Cakes", 1993
Lock back folder. Damascus blade, bolsters, and back spring. File worked on blade, back spring, and liners. Pearl handles, lanyard-ring lock release.
Overall length 6 1/8" (156 mm).
Kaj Embretsen, Sweden
Lock Back Folder, 2004
Three-bar Damascus blade and bolsters, 14k gold bail and pins. File worked back spring and liners, stag handle.
Overall length 6 3/4" (171 mm).

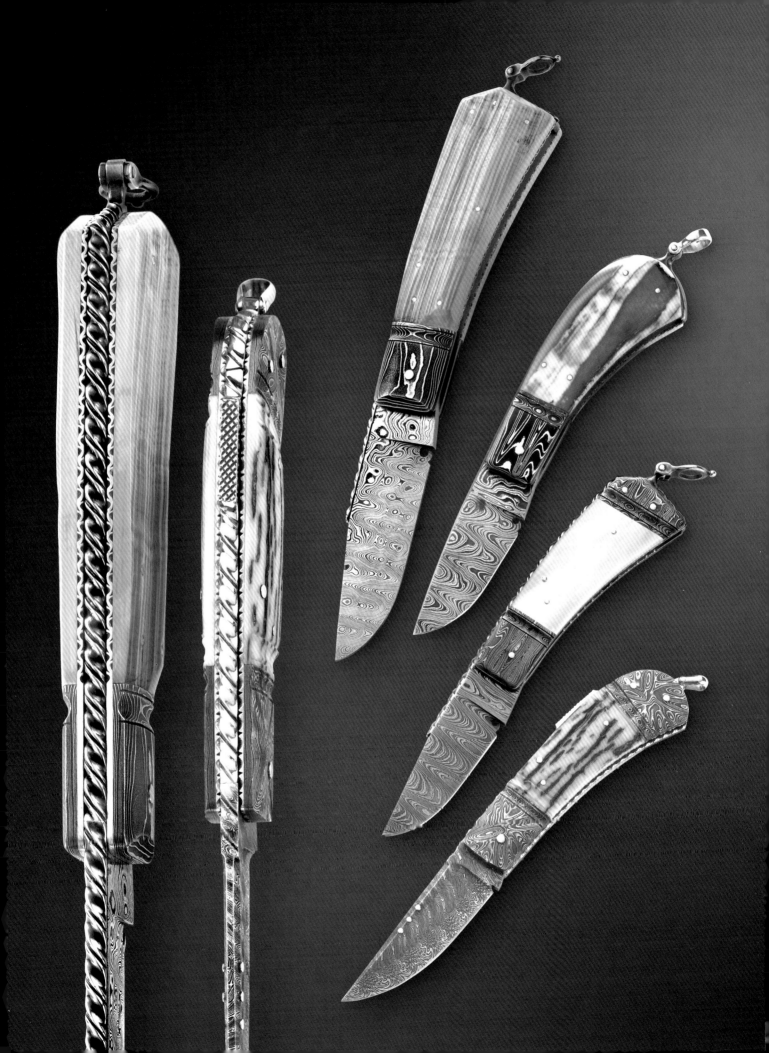

Ed Wormser *USA*

Opposite page, from the top:
Bob Loveless, USA
"5 Piece Loveless set", early '90s
"Drop Point Hunter", "Caper
Finn", "Straight Hunter", "Utility"
and "Semi Skinner", all with
matching premium stag handles.
Bolsters engraved and carved
by Shaw Lebowitz (USA) with 5
different animals representing the
American Big Five.
Overall lengths 8 1/4" (210 mm).

I was in Milan, Italy, in l992, and I just happened to stumble into a store called Lorenzi. I had never before seen such beautiful knives. I noticed that the knife makers were American. I bought one knife, came home and found some dealers who sold knives by the same makers I had discovered in Milan. I then went to the Blade Show, and it was full speed ahead. A few years later, I decided to turn my passion for collecting into a business. I became partners in the New York Custom Knife Show. I now run the Chicago Custom Knife Show, www.chicagocustomknifeshow.com, which takes place in September, and the Tactical Invitational Knife Show, which has been held in Las Vegas for the past two years. The custom knife world is a wonderful place, full of artists and collectors all having a lot of fun with their passions. I enjoy being part of it, and my goal is to expand this world by bringing more people into the hobby.

Left, from the top:
Michael Walker, USA
"Blade Lock Zipper", mid '90s
Titanium handles, engraved by Patricia
Walker (USA).
Overall length 7 3/4" (197 mm).
*"This may be the most beautiful knife in
my entire collection".*
"Blade Lock Double Zipper", early '90s
Titanium handles, engraved by Patricia
Walker (USA).
*"The symmetrical double zipper on the
dagger blade is a very unusual feature".*
Overall length 7 1/2" (195 mm).

Opposite page, from the top:
Michael Walker, USA
"Crescent Shape Zipper", mid '90s
Tiny blade lock with zipper blade,
stainless Damascus blade and bolsters.
Overall length 5" (127 mm).
"Blade Lock Zipper", 2003
Stainless Damascus blade and bolsters.
Meteorite handle with
gold accents.
Overall length 7 3/4" (197 mm).
"Blade Lock Zipper", late '90s
Stainless Damascus blade and bolsters.
Gold and mixed metal
inlays in handle.
Overall length 7 3/4" (197 mm).
"Blade Lock Zipper", 2002
Stainless Damascus blade and bolsters.
Gold and mixed metal
inlays in handle.
Overall length 7 3/4" (197 mm).
"Small Blade Lock Zipper", 2001
Stainless Damascus blade and bolsters.
Gold and mixed metal
inlays in handle.
Overall length 6 1/4" (159 mm).

Left, from the top:
Ray and Ron Appleton, USA
"Infilock", early '90s
The knife locks up in an infinite
number of positions.
*"This is one of my favorites. Great
to look at and even better to hold in
the hand".*
Overall length 7 1/2" (195 mm).
"Button lock" (Ray), late '80s
Overall length 5 3/4" (146 mm).
"IQ mechanism" (Ray), early '90s
Overall length 6 1/2" (165 mm).
"Push-Dagger" (Ray), mid '90s
The knife opens and locks in 3
different positions, becoming a push
dagger in one position.
Overall length 6 1/2" (165 mm).

Opposite page, from the top:
Jim Schmidt, USA
"Wildflowers" 3 piece set, 1991
Stag handles, Damascus blades
and bolsters.
*"This may be the only set Jim
Schmidt ever made".*
Overall lengths 9" (229 mm),
8" (203 mm), 7" (178 mm).
"Night Sugar", 1993
Mastodon ivory handle, Damascus
blade and bolster.
Overall length 8" (203 mm)
"Puff O Smoke", 1998
Spectacular mastodon ivory handle,
Damascus blade and bolster,
14k gold liners.
*"This is probably the nicest piece of
ivory I have ever seen on a knife".*
Overall length 7" (178 mm).

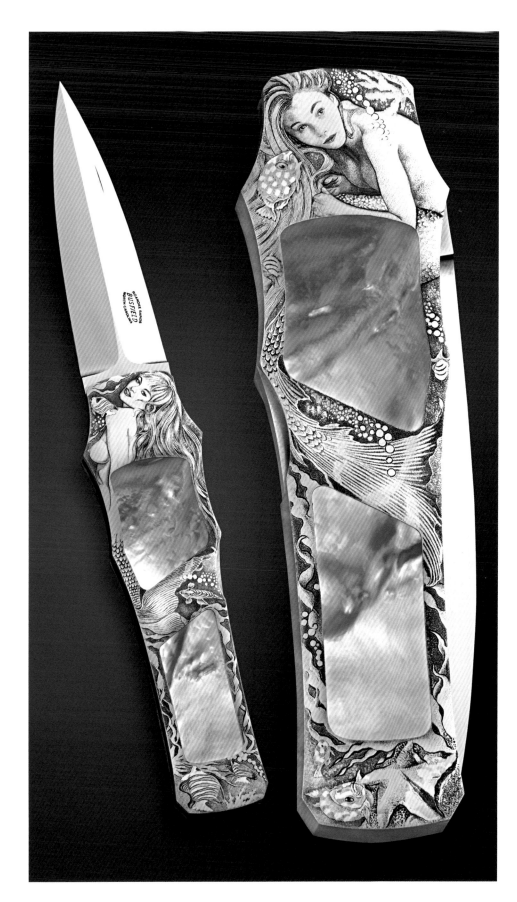

On the left:
Jack Busfield, USA, *2003*
Double Mother-of-Pearl interframes.
Engraved by Creative Art.
Overall length 8" (203 mm).

Opposite page, from the top:
Scott Sawby, USA, *1999*
Engraved by Manrico Torcoli (Italy).
Overall length 7 1/2" (195 mm).
Steve Hoel, USA, *2003*
Engraved by Francesco Amatori
(Italy).
Overall length 7" (178 mm).
Kaj Embretsen, Sweden, *2002*
Damascus blade and bolster with
scrimshaw of polar bears by
Francesco Amatori (Italy).
*"This is the first time I ever saw
scrimshaw done on pearl".*
Overall length 8" (203 mm).

Left, from the top:
Bill Moran, USA
"Three Quillon daggers",
1978-1985
Curly Maple handle with
fluted and twisted sterling
silver wire inlaid sheath is curly
maple with silver wire work and
an ivory tip.
Overall length 11 3/4" (298 mm).
Ebony handle
Overall length 15 1/2" (394 mm).
Ebony handle
Overall length 13 1/2" (343 mm).

Opposite page, from the top:
Bill Moran, USA
"Lock Back Folder", late '80s
Damascus blade, ivory handle.
Overall length 9" (229 mm).
"Lock Back Folder", early '90s
Curly maple handle, with silver
wire inlay.
Overall length 9" (229 mm).
"Slip Joint Folder", late '70s
Ivory handle.
Overall length 8 3/4" (222 mm).
"Lock Back Folder", early '80s
Ebony handle.
Overall length 8 3/4" (222 mm).

Opposite page, from the left:
Bill Moran, USA
"Giant ST 23", late '70s
Damascus blade and curly maple
handle with *"kill em all and let God
sort em out"* in silver wire inlay.
Overall length 17" (432 mm).
"St 24/ST 23 Combination Knife", 1974
ST 24 Damascus blade with an ST 23
curly maple handle.
Overall length 14 1/2" (368 mm).
"ST 23", early '80s
Damascus blade and curly maple
handle with silver wire inlay. Curly
maple sheath with silver wire inlay
and ivory throat and tip.
Overall length 12 1/2" (mm).

Right, from the top:
Bill Moran, USA
"Featherweight Utility Knife", mid '70s
Damascus blade and curly maple
handle inlaid with silver wire.
Overall length 7 3/4" (197 mm).
"Jamblya", mid '80s
Damascus blade and curly maple
handle inlaid with silver wire. Curly
maple sheath inlaid with silver wire,
has ivory tip.
Overall length 12" (317 mm).

This page:
Bob Loveless, USA
"Amber Stag Handle Set", 2005
Three knives with matching amber stag handles, all of them carrying double naked lady logos.
Overall lengths: **"Big Bear"** 14" (356 mm), **"Junior Bear"** 11" (279 mm), **"Chute"** 9" (229 mm).

Opposite page, from the left:
Bob Loveless, USA
"Three Big Bear Sub Hilt Fighters"
Stag handle Big Bear, made in 2005, has the double naked lady logo. **Sheep horn Big Bear**, made in the late '80s, was engraved by Dan Wilkinson and has the Riverside logo. **Ivory micarta Big Bear**, made in 1973, has the Lawndale logo. All three knives have 8 1/2" (216 mm) blades and overall lengths of 14" (356 mm).

Left, from the top:
Ron Lake, USA
"Two Knives", early '90s
One with stag interframe, the other with with tortoise shell interframe. Engraved by Steve Lindsay (USA).
Overall lengths 4 3/4" (121 mm).
"Gold Knife", early '90s
Black-lip pearl interframe engraved by Sam Alfano (USA).
Overall length 6" (152 mm).
"Mother-of-Pearl Interframe", 2003
Stainless steel knife with amazing artistic coverage. Engraving on the steel bolsters and scrimshaw on the pearl interframes, all done by Francesco Amatori (Italy).
Overall length 7 1/4" (184 mm).

Opposite page, from the top:
Bob Loveless, USA
"Semi Skinner", 2003
Long bolster with hidden pins. Amber stag handles. Double naked lady logo. Engraved by Manrico Torcoli (Italy).
Overall length 8" (203 mm).
"Straight Hunter", mid '90s
Long bolster with hidden pins. Red micarta handles. Double naked lady logo. Engraved by Manrico Torcoli (Italy).
Overall length 10 1/2" (267 mm).
"Semi Skinner", 2001
Long bolster with hidden pins. Amber stag handles. Riverside logo. Engraved by Ron Skaggs (USA).
Overall length 8" (203 mm).
"Drop Point Hunter", 2001
Long bolster with hidden pins. Amber stag handles. Engraved by Ron Skaggs (USA). Double naked lady logo.
Overall length 8" (203 mm).

On the left:

Ron Lake, USA

"Two stag interframes", 1998

A set of two stag tail lock
interframes with deep relief
engraving by Firmo Fracassi
(Italy).
Overall lengths 6 1/4" (159 mm).

Opposite page, from the top:

Buster Warenski, USA

"Ruby Dagger", 2003

Handle fashioned from
a single ruby crystal. Fittings
are blued steel with 24k
gold inlays and rings of
nickel-silver set with rubies.
Engraving, sculpting, and
stone setting by
Julie Warenski (USA).
Overall length 17" (432 mm).

"Kukri", 1998

Lapis handle. Gold inlays,
engraving and sculpting by
Julie Warenski (USA).
Overall length 22" (559 mm).

Opposite page:
Owen Wood and Amayak Stepanyan, USA
"Spirit of Horta", 2006
A liner lock. Blade steel is Owen Wood's Pinstripe and Herringbone Damascus. The two elements are carefully chosen to create a blade that is integrated with the overall design. The pinstripe is made from pure nickel layers alternated with 1095 high carbon spring steel. The edge is a 1095/15N20 explosion pattern Damascus. Fluted stainless steel Damascus bolsters. The pivot is inlaid with Black-lip pearl. 416 stainless steel scales are carved and engraved by Amayak Stepanyan in an Art-Nouveau style inspired by the work of the Belgian architect and designer Victor Horta (1861-1947). The collector's initials and the names of both maker and engraver are added to the design. The edges of the titanium liners are carefully rounded and stand proud of the scales, bolsters and back spacer. Anodized, the liners create a gold border around the handle, adding delightful sparkle to the design. The 303 stainless steel back spacer is decorated with a diamond pattern and electro chemically blued. Overall length 5 3/4" (146 mm).

Thinking back to the hot night in August 2001, when this pretentious project was conceived, usually brings forth a strange mixture of emotions. All I actually wanted and dreamed for was to have a series of quality books, that between their covers would encompass the various aspects of the art of modern custom knives. I wanted books that had many quality illustrations but also comprehensive background texts, detailed descriptions of all the knives and an insight into the "behind the scenes" of custom knifemaking. For many years I purchased almost every book published in English dealing with custom knives, but never found anything remotely like what I really wanted to have.

Eventually, as nobody else met the challenge, and digital photography and global communications reached the required quality, I decided to pick up the glove and do something about my dream. It was time to contact some of the prominent custom knifemakers around the world and plunge into the adventure of a lifetime. Then, one year later, I met Paolo Saviolo. He believed in my vision with all his heart and took it to the next level by introducing it to the world.

I always wonder how I could have even imagined that a series of books of this magnitude could be dealt with and completed in one's lifetime. Not only that, but completed while sitting at home with my Macintosh and a telephone. That is one thought that often goes through my mind after which I immediately turn to the bookshelf and check to make sure that all this did actually happen. Then, as usual, I end up with a sweet feeling of accomplishment, the joy of having these four books on a shelf, in my study, and knowing that many thousands are also enjoying them all over the world, just as I do. Four books, five years, and I have a feeling that this is just the beginning...

ddd

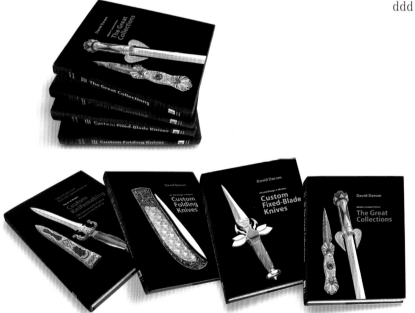

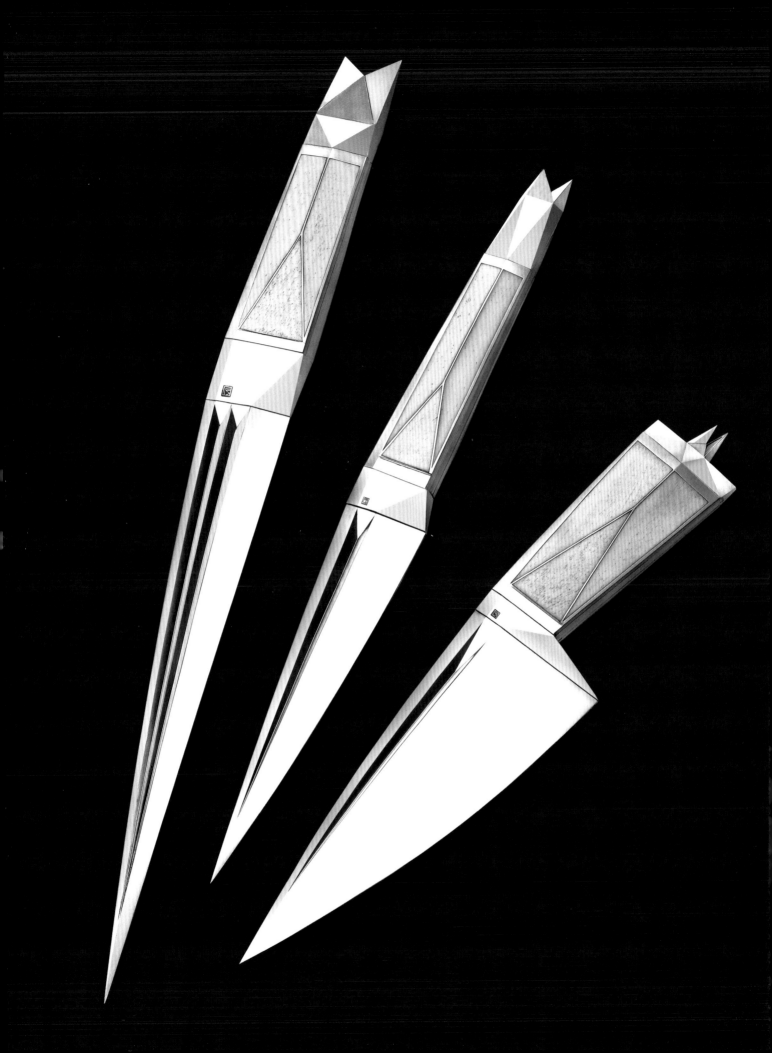

Knifemaker Index

Opposite page:

Jurgen Steinau, Germany
"Ivory Set", 1991

A unique set of three fixed-blade knives with elephant ivory inlays. Overall lengths 11 7/16" (290 mm), 9 1/16" (230 mm) and 8 1/4" (210 mm).
From the collection of Luigi Peppini, Italy

Opposite page, from the left:
"Three Daggers"
Willie Rigney, USA, **1991**
Dagger with Charolite handle and engraving by Old Dominion and David Perdue.
Overall length 14" (356 mm).
Buster Warenski, USA, 1999
Fiber optic handle, engraved by Julie Warenski.
Overall length 15 1/2" (394 mm).
Jim Ence, USA,
"Gladiator", 2000
Dagger with 6 white sapphires and 15 emralds, 24k gold with fossil walrus ivory.
Overall length 17 1/2" (444 mm).
All three knives are from the collection of Dave Nittinger, USA

Opposite page, from the left:
Owen Wood and Amayak Stepanyan, USA
"Art Deco Liner Lock", 2006
Blade material is Owen Wood Pinstripe and Explosion Damascus, bolsters are Damasteel, liners are titanium. Brown-lip pearl inlay in the stainless steel pivot. Deep relief engraving in Art Deco style by Amayak Stepanyan. Overall length 4 3/4" (120 mm).
From the collection of Don Guild, Hawaii.

"Metropolis", 2006
A double action automatic liner lock folder. Blade material is Owen Wood Pinstripe and Explosion composite Damascus. Damasteel bolsters, titanium liners and Black-lip pearl scales. Deep relief engraving in Art Deco style by Amayak Stepanyan. Overall Length 7 1/8" (180 mm).
From the collection of Don Guild, Hawaii.

"Persian Folder", 2006
Liner lock folding knife in Persian style. Blade material is Owen Wood Herringbone with right and left twist composite Damascus. 18k gold bolsters, titanium liners and Black-lip pearl scales. Deep relief engraving in Art Nouveau style by Amayak Stepanyan. Overall Length 7 1/8" (180 mm).

Opposite page, from the left:

From the collection of Gary Hoy, USA

Kenny Steigerwalt, USA
"Automatic button lock", 1990
Robert Eggerling Mosaic Damascus blade and bolsters. Fancy file worked liners and back bar with scalloped bolsters. Mammoth scales. Overall length 8 3/4" (222 mm).

Steve Hill, USA
"One-handed Liner Lock", 2004
Sapphire thumb stud. Robert Eggerling Spider-web Damascus blade. Eggerling blued Damascus bolsters. Mammoth ivory scales, blue anodized, file worked, titanium liners. Overall length 8 1/2" (216 mm).

Donald Vogt, USA
"Automatic Liner Lock", 1995-1997
Black-lip pearl button. Devin Thomas Raindrop Damascus blade, Eggerling Leaf pattern Damascus carved bolsters. Extensively carved Mother-of-Pearl handle with gold pins and bail. Gold anodized and file worked titanium liners. Gold-lip pearl inlaid into back bar. Overall length 11" (279 mm).

Shaun and Sharla Hansen, USA
"Folding Dagger", 2004
Sole authorship, liner lock, interframe, folding dagger. The blade is Shaun's Turkish Damascus, forged to shape, carved and gold inlaid. The handle is fully engraved, gold inlaid, carved and French grayed. The Bulino engraving is of a beautiful maiden on one side and a knight riding to her rescue on the other. The interframe inlays are brown agate. Overall length 9 7/8" (251 mm).

Shaun and Sharla Hansen, USA
"One handed Liner Lock", 1998
Amethyst thumb stud. Shaun's own Star Pattern Damascus blade and bolsters. Blue anodized and file worked titanium liners. Carved Gold-lip pearl handles and inlays in back bar. Overall length 7" (178 mm).

Born in 1948, in Central PA, I became a Journeyman Tool and Die Maker in 1976, making forge dies at a local brass company. In 1977 I started working at Penn State University and for twenty years made experimental propellers for Torpedoes and Submarines for the Dept. of the Navy. In 1997 I transferred to the Physics Dept. where I taught students how to run Machine Shop machines. I retired from Penn State in 2003. Twenty five years ago I started collecting factory knives, (Case, Gerber, etc.). I have since sold or traded all of my factory knives and collect only custom, handmade one of a kind art knives. There are presently over 70 knives in my collection.

Related Books

Allara Roberto, **Hand-crafted Knives, Masterpieces of American Knifemakers**, Priuli and Verlucca, 1999

Allara Roberto, **The World of Custom Knives**, Tipografia Edizioni Saviolo, 2001

Darom David, Dr., **Art and Design in Modern Custom Folding Knives**, DDD and Tipografia Edizioni Saviolo, 2003

Darom David, Dr., **Art and Design in Modern Custom Fixed-Blade Knives**, DDD and Tipografia Edizioni Saviolo, 2005

Darom David, Dr. and Dennis Greenbaum, **The Art of Modern Custom Knifemaking**, DDD and Tipografia Edizioni Saviolo, 2006

Fowler Ed, **Knife Talk**, Krause Publications, 1998

Kertzman Joe, 26th Annual **KNIVES 2006**, Krause Publications, 2005

Kertzman Joe, 27th Annual **KNIVES 2007**, Krause Publications, 2006

Pohl Dietmar, **Tactical Knives, Designs, Manufacturers, Applications**, Krause Publications, 2003

Schroen Karl, **The Hand Forged Knife**, Knife World Publications, 1985

Terzuola Bob, **The Tactical Folding Knife**, Krause Publications, 2000

Weyer Jim, **Knives: Points of Interest**, Weyer International, Part I (1984), Part II (1987), Part III (1990), Part IV (1993), Part V (1999)

Opposite page:
Stefan Steigerwald, Germany
www.steigerwald-messer.de
"Arctic Hunt", 2006
A folding knife made of hand-forged Schneider Damascus, hardened to 58 Rc. The detailed carving and engraving was done by Charles Roulin from Switzerland, showing a boat with armed Inuits hunting, surrounded by narwhales, polar bears, seals and penguins. Birds are flying in the sky, searching for remains from a successful hunt. The whole scene is complete when the folder is closed. The blade is locked with a central-lock and has a gold inlay with the makers and the project name. A sapphire is inlaid on the opening button and over 80 pieces of lapis-lazuli were ground and fitted in the handle. On the back, there is a hidden mechanism for a lanyard loop.
Not shown is the wooden box made of ebony, desert ironwood and bronze. It has a magnifying glass and built-in illumination to enable easy viewing of the engraving and carving. The 3 15/16" (100 mm) blade is 3/16" (4.8 mm) thick.
Overall length 9 1/4" (235 mm).

Contact Information

The Author

Dr. David Darom

1, Haim Bajayo Street
Jerusalem 93145, Israel
Phone: (+972) 2 566 5885
Cellphone: (+972) 522 602345
email: ddd@cc.huji.ac.il
www.david-darom.com

Series producer and distributor

Paolo Saviolo

Tipografia Edizioni Saviolo snc
Via Col di Lana, 12
13100 - Vercelli, Italy
Phone: (+39) 0161-391000
Fax: (+39) 0161-271256
email: paolo@savioloedizioni.it
psaviolo@tin.it
www.savioloedizioni.it

Saviolo Publisher USA

Mandeville, Louisiana 70470-2675
United State of America
Phone: (985) 792-0115
email: ssj@saviolopublisher.com
www.saviolopublisher.com

"The River That Carries Us"
Hilton Purvis
P. O. Box 371, Noordhoek, 7979,
South Africa
Phone/Fax: (+27) 21 7891114
email: hiltonp@telkomsa.net

"The Dress Tactical Folding Knife"
Neil Ostroff
"TNK" - True North Knives
797 Bertrand Circle Saint Laurent,
Quebec, Canada H4M 1W1
Phone: (514) 748-9985
email: neil@truenorthknives.com
www.truenorthknives.com

Darrel Ralph, USA
c/o BRIAR INDUSTRIES
4185 S. St. Rt. 605, Galena,
OH 43021, USA
Phone: (740) 965-9970
email: info@darrelralph.com
www.darrelralph.com

Ken Onion, Hawaii
email: ken@kenonionknives.com
www.kenonionknives.com

Phil Boguszewski, USA
P. O. Box 99329
Lakewood, Washington 98499, USA
Phone: (253) 581-7096
email: knives01@aol.com

Greg Lightfoot, Canada
RR#2, Kitskoty, AB T0B 2P0, Canada
Phone: (780) 846-2812
email: pitbull@lightfootknives.com
www.lightfootknives.com

Mick Strider, USA
Strider Knives, Inc.
120 N. Pacific St. Unit L-7
San Marcos, CA 92069 USA
Phone: (760) 471-8275
Fax: (503) 218-7069
email: striderguys@striderknives.com
www.striderknives.com

Pat and Wes Crawford, USA
Crawford Knives, LLC
205 N. Center Drive
West Memphis, AR 72301
Phone/Fax: (870) 732-2452
email: patcrawford1@earthlink.net
www.crawfordknives.com

Opposite page, from the left:
Koji Hara, Japan, *2001/2002*
Two Integral fixed-blade knives with numerous
abalone shell inlays and boot blades.
Overall lengths 7 7/8" (200 mm) and 6" (152 mm).
From the collection of Dr. Pierluigi Peroni, Italy.

C. Gray Taylor, USA

Taylor became fascinated with knives after seeing the movie "The Iron Mistress" (the story of Jim Bowie). He sold his first knife in 1975, attended his first Knifemaker's Guild show in 1976, in Dallas, made his first multi blade folder in the early '80s and started making knives full-time after retiring in 1997. Taylor is a member of the Art Knife Invitational, a prestigious group of 25 of the most collectible knifemakers in the world. Nowadays he usually makes traditional multi-blade lobster folders and historical pieces.

"Sleeveboard Lobster Pattern with Scissors", 2006

ATS-34 blades, manicure blade, and scissors. 14k gold liners, bolsters, raised pins, and bale. The scissors have a gold screw, and gold spring wire. The antique tortoise handles were inlaid with 14k pink, green, white and yellow gold by the maker. Closed length 2 5/8" (67 mm), fully opened 6 1/4" (159 mm).

"The knife was made as a special project for a good customer. It was an anniversary gift for his wife of 27 years".